An Outline of Piaget's Developmental Psychology for Students and Teachers

by Ruth M. Beard

Senior Lecturer in
Higher Education,
University of London Institute of
Education

LONDON

ROUTLEDGE & KEGAN PAUL

First published 1969
by Routledge & Kegan Paul Ltd
Broadway House, 68-74 Carter Lane
London, EC4V 5EL

Reprinted 1969, 1970, 1971, 1972

Printed in Great Britain
by Northumberland Press Limited
Gateshead

ISBN 0 7100 6340 7 (c)
ISBN 0 7100 6344 X (p)

THE STUDENTS LIBRARY OF EDUCATION has been designed to meet the needs of students of Education at Colleges of Education and at University Institutes and Departments. It will also be valuable for practising teachers and educationists. The series takes full account of the latest developments in teacher-training and of new methods and approaches in education. Separate volumes will provide authoritative and up-to-date accounts of the topics within the major fields of sociology, philosophy and history of education, educational psychology, and method. Care has been taken that specialist topics are treated lucidly and usefully for the non-specialist reader. Altogether, the Students Library of Education will provide a comprehensive introduction and guide to anyone concerned with the study of education, and with educational theory and practice.

J. W. TIBBLE

No one in recent years has made a greater impact on educational thought and research than Jean Piaget. His contributions to the fields of genetic epistemology and intellectual development are now recognized as the most important to have been made in this century.

Yet the impact of his work on educational practice is less than it ought to have been and ought to be. Nearly everyone in education nowadays talks about Piaget. Rather fewer understand his work and fewer still design their work with children according to its principles. In part this is due to the sheer difficulty of the field in which Piaget has done his pioneer work, in part at least it is due to the fact that he is not himself the clearest of writers. His work stands in need of effective exposition and comment, particularly for students of education.

Dr. Beard's 'Outline' admirably fulfils this need. Here is a lucid account of the major features of Piaget's work which is of interest to teachers. It has been carefully arranged and expressed, with plenty of telling illustrations, yet it is an account which does not seek to hide the genuine complexity of the issues with which Piaget deals.

BEN MORRIS

v

Acknowledgements

Since one of the chief criticisms of Piaget's work is that it is difficult to read, I have asked a number of students, and others as yet unacquainted with psychologists' jargon, to read and comment on this book or sections of it. For this service I wish to thank, firstly, the group of science and mathematics graduates to whom I was tutor in the School of Education, University of Birmingham, 1964-65; it was their puzzled frowns over what I supposed was a lucid Chapter 1 which obliged me to simplify the style and to increase the number of illustrations. Secondly, I should like to thank readers who had no prior knowledge of educational psychology, my secretaries Elizabeth Bull and Lysbeth Hill and my niece Sarah Davies, whose comments led to further minor modifications until they judged the text clear and easy to follow.

The book also benefited from the criticisms of Margaret Spencer, who has worked with Jean Piaget, and of Professor P. E. Vernon and Professor J. W. Tibble. Several inconsistencies have been drawn to my attention by Professor Ben Morris, editor of the Psychology section in the Students Library of Education. I am very grateful to them all for the care with which they read it.

Finally I should like to thank Elizabeth Bull, Lysbeth Hill and Angela Harley for the speed and accuracy with which they typed successive versions of the text.

R.M.B

Contents

Glossary

Accommodation: modification of schemas as a result of new experiences.

Adaptation: a balance between accommodation and assimilation resulting in adjustment to the environment.

Animism: attribution of consciousness to objects.

Artificialism: belief that natural events are caused by, or for, human activity.

Assimilation: incorporation of new objects and experiences into existing schemas.

Circular reaction: active reproduction of a result at first obtained by chance, with variations and experimentation.

Cognitive processes: mental processes concerned with knowing, such as perception, memory, imagery, reasoning, etc.

Concept: idea of a class of objects, or a relation, normally expressed by a word.

Conservation: invariance of quantity, e.g. of substance under change of shape, of length on change of direction or position, etc.

Egocentricity: distortive interpretation of other people's experiences, and actions or persons or objects, in terms of the individual's own schemas.

Euclidean geometry: a quantitative branch of geometry,

concerned with measurement of lines, angles, surfaces and volumes.

Group of displacements: reversible sequences of actions coordinated to achieve a desired end.

Image: a revived sense experience without sensory stimulation.

Intellectual realism: inaccurate representation of an object due to reading into the situation what the child knows instead of limiting it to what he can perceive.

Internalization: representation of the external world by memories, images, language and symbols.

Intuitive stage: the stage in which children appear to make immediate judgments without conscious mental steps in their formulation.

Juxtaposition: linking together of successive, unrelated judgments, views or explanations.

Operation: an action which takes place in imagination.

Perception: process of becoming immediately aware of something through the senses.

Pre-concept: a schema in which a type individual is used to represent a group of objects in some ways resembling it.

Projective geometry: the geometry of transforming one line or surface into another as in making plane maps of the earth. Used here of shadows and sections.

Realism: extension of the speaker's view to all possible points of view: a kind of immediate, but illegitimate, generalization.

Representational schema: a schema in which one thing is used to represent another.

Reversible action: an action which can be retraced by an opposite action.

Reversible operation: an operation which can be annulled by an inverse operation.

Schema: a well defined sequence of physical or mental actions.

Sensori-motor: simultaneously perceptual and motor.

Sign: a collective symbol, such as a number, letter or word.

Symbol: an image evoked mentally, or a material object chosen to represent a class of actions or objects.

Syncretism: linking together of unrelated things or ideas.

Topology: the geometry of position, relating to boundaries, order, intersections and closure.

Transduction: 'reasoning' by direct analogy, from particular to particular, without generalization or logical rigour.

Introduction

This is a book for students and teachers who wish to know more about Piaget's work but who find it too difficult, or time-consuming, to read much in the original. Its purpose is two-fold: both to make some of his ideas and observations available fairly quickly to the reader, and to introduce most of his special vocabulary, so facilitating reading in the original. It is true that there are already three books by psychologists which are entirely, or mainly, concerned with Piaget's findings; but one deals only with concepts in mathematics and science (Lovell, 1961), a second (Peel, 1960) is more general but is found difficult by many students, and the third (Flavell, 1963) is too long and comprehensive to serve as an introduction. All three texts may be found valuable as supplementary reading. There is, in addition, a brief but excellent article (Mays, 1955) (though too brief, of course, to be comprehensive) which does not make use of Piaget's sometimes confusing vocabulary.

In this volume the author attempts in the space of some thirty thousand words, to outline Piaget's theories of the development of children's thinking as well as to give a representative sample of his many observations and experiments with children. Inevitably there are omissions; for example, there is no attempt to outline Piaget's discussions of his own theories in relation to those of other schools of psychology. But, since this is a book for teachers, reference is made to similar investigations which have somewhat different findings. For instance, differences between results for English-speaking children and those tested by Piaget or his collaborators are mentioned.

The importance of Piaget's work lies both in the method and its extent. His 'clinical' method of investigating children's thinking is exceptional in that he seeks reasons for children's beliefs and opinions. It involves conversations with each child, which differ according to the replies given, so that the quality of thinking in each case can be assessed regardless of whether an answer is 'right' or 'wrong'. Some critics have objected that a long series of questions may oblige a child to give an answer which he does not believe; but, like psychiatrists who claim that patients' inventions are as revealing as their descriptions of events, Piaget may claim that this too tells us something about a child's level of thinking.

The extent of Piaget's investigations vastly exceeds that of any previous inquiries into children's thinking. By means of observations and experiments with his own three children he followed the cognitive development of infants; two books cover these investigations (Piaget, 1953a+b). A further book describes the origins of play and imitation in children as symbolic ways of representing the world are learned (Piaget, 1960). With children of school age, sometimes with the aid of collaborators, he studied the development of language and thought in children (Piaget, 1926), their judgments and reasoning (Piaget, 1928), their understanding of physical causality (Piaget, 1930) and origins of phenomena in the world (Piaget, 1929). The last four books, with a fifth concerning the development of moral concepts (Piaget, 1932), were his earliest books, dating from the 1920s. His methods of investigation were criticized then by English and American psychologists as being too exclusively verbal. Subsequently a very valuable series of investigations showed an increase in number of experiments to be discussed or tasks to be performed by the children. It includes investigations into the development of concepts of number (Piaget and Szeminska, 1952), time (Piaget, 1946), speed and movement (Piaget, 1946a), quantity (Piaget, 1941), space (Piaget, 1956), geometry (Piaget, 1960), and classification (Piaget, 1959). In 1950 *The Psychology of Intelligence* was published in English. This gives an account of Piaget's theory of the origins of intelligence in children and the stages they pass through in cognitive development. Recently, Piaget and Inhelder have given more attention to adolescent thinking (Inhelder and Piaget, 1959), and, in an untranslated volume, they have summarized the periods of cognitive development and their characteristics (Piaget, 1956). Again more recently, Piaget with some of his students has made more than thirty studies of perception which are listed by Flavell (1963).

Despite its length this list is by no means the sum total of Piaget's publications. None of his very numerous articles has been listed and some of his books have been omitted, but in so brief a text it is not possible to make reference to them all.

There are certain difficulties in following Piaget's results and conclusions which do not stem from the lack of clarity in style of which many readers complain; they arise chiefly from the absence of a statistical basis to his work. Piaget claims that this is not possible since different questions were asked from each child so that their responses are not strictly comparable. However, other investigators following his 'clinical' method have assigned children's answers to stages, or have described levels of thinking somewhat different from those described by Piaget, and have related these levels with age, mental age, sex or other relevant data, as well as giving an exact description of the samples of children used in their investigations. To teachers it is of some importance not only to know the order of stages in thinking, if there is an invariable order, but also to know what misconceptions to expect among children of different ages and at what age the majority of children in a given environment reach each stage. Such information is valuable as a guide to teaching methods. Where it is available it is mentioned in the text and implications for teaching are further discussed at the conclusions of chapters.

To ensure that the text of the monograph was well suited to the readers for whom it was intended, some teachers and students were asked to read drafts and to comment on them. As a result of their criticisms the number of observations and experiments reported has been increased. So far as possible these precede discussion of the nature of children's thinking which accounts for the difficulties displayed in their answers. However, in Chapter 1 the developmental theory is outlined and many terms are already explained and defined since they are constantly required in subsequent chapters. The reader may find it a condensed and rather difficult chapter. If so, he is recommended to read it quickly and to return to it as a summary at the end.

1

The development of intelligence

Introduction

A typical problem for a test of reasoning for the 11+ age
group requires them to find a 'missing' letter, figure or
object among a collection. Such a test requires that they
should see the common characteristics of a class, or the
nature of a series, in order to deduce the missing entity.
In the problem at the head of the chapter the difficulty
lies in spotting the basis on which the letters must be
classified in order to make a reasonable correspondence.
Have you noticed that I, V and X are Roman numbers?
If so you have an ability to recognize these letters as
symbols for numbers and, implicitly, you have matched
letters one-to-one with the sequence of numbers they

represent. I the symbol for one is opposite *A*, X is opposite the tenth letter, *J*; opposite V it must be the fifth letter which is missing viz. *E*. Again numbers are matched with letters, both being understood to be ordered sequences. Incidentally appreciation of a one-to-one correspondence is involved and a relationship—that of 'opposite to'—has been used.

Were we born with these abilities? Observation of small children learning letters or numbers suggests that we were not. But until Piaget and his collaborators made a detailed study of the development of children's thinking from birth to adolescence, it was believed that some perceptions at least, or a sense of time, or even some concepts might be inborn. In following Piaget's work we shall find that children learn only slowly to recognize shapes and sizes, while in infancy they do not even realize that objects are permanent.

Piaget considers that certain processes underlie all learning, whether in simple organisms or in human beings. The two essential processes are on the one hand, *adaptation* to the environment and, on the other, *organization* of experience by means of action, memory, perceptions, or other kinds of mental activities. But, whereas in a simple organism adaptation is a matter of living to satisfy elementary needs and organization is rudimentary, the human child, as he develops, adapts to a succession of environments and with increasing complexity of organization.

Basic cognitive processes

From observations and experiments with his own three children Piaget concluded that at birth infants were endowed with only a few reflexes, such as sucking and grasping, and innate tendencies to exercise the reflexes and to organize their actions. In other words, the infants did not inherit any ready-made mental abilities but only a manner of responding to the environment. In essentials this response consisted in an urge to adapt to the environment, as any living creature must if it is to survive.

The first evidence of capacity to organize appeared in the development of habitual actions. Very soon after birth each infant tended to seek with its mouth anything which made contact with its lips, and to grasp any object which touched the palm of the hand. In the case of Piaget's son, Laurent, the tendency to grasp developed very early into a habit of clasping and unclasping his hands. Such well-defined sequences of actions Piaget terms *schemas* or *schemata*. Their chief characteristic, whatever their nature or complexity, is that they are organized wholes which are frequently repeated and which can be recognized easily among other diverse and varying behaviours.

So soon as a schema of action is developed it is applied to every new object, and in every new situation; the infant sucks an increasing variety of objects as his range of action widens, for example. Piaget's term for the process of incorporating new objects or experiences into existing schemas is *assimilation*. Whereas an organism assimilates its environment chiefly by taking in food and digesting it, a child, in addition, assimilates experiences into a succession of cognitive schemas. The young infant has schemas only of actions and perceptions, but later a child represents one thing by another, using words and symbols, and so constructs *representational schemas*. However, a young child commonly distorts information to fit his point of view: he attributes life and feeling to objects, or supposes that natural phenomena such as mountains and lakes are man-made. Piaget considers that this is because young children assimilate new observations to schemas derived from their own actions and experiences. Their play also is largely a process of assimilating new objects and experiences into phantasies.

Even with an increased range of representational schemas in later childhood, when games of pretence disappear, assimilation still has a distorting character with

3

unfamiliar and difficult material. The pre-adolescent who cannot understand proverbs because he does not yet abstract common meanings in different statements, attempts to assimilate them to some familiar experience. For example, (Piaget, 1926, Ec. 9;1) equates 'By wielding his hammer a blacksmith learns his trade' with 'Men should be rewarded or punished according to what they have done', and explains this 'equivalence' by saying 'because if we learn our trade properly, we are rewarded, and if we don't we are punished'.

Thus, although assimilation extends the range of a schema by incorporating new objects and experiences it may fail to do so in a manner which is generally meaningful. Nevertheless, the child has striven to organize the new data by some means intelligible to him, and this will be modified in time by new experiences and through discussion with other people.

Complementary to the process of assimilation is the process of seeking new successful modes of behaviour when the environment does not respond to the schemas already learned by the child. Thus an infant who has learned to pull stoppers from bottles finds a screw top perplexing until he discovers by trial and error that it must be turned. An older child asked to balance a single weight by a double one on a Meccano strip balance may also use trial and error entirely but he will learn more quickly. An adolescent is likely to try to think out a solution to an unfamiliar problem, consciously combining schemas or modifying them. This process of modifying schemas to solve problems arising from new experiences within the environment Piaget calls *accommodation*. Except in very young infants accommodation is an active process which displays itself in exploration, questioning, trial and error, making experiments or by reflection; combinations of schemas are tried out, or experiments are made and information sought, until the learner arrives at successful new schemas.

4

Through the interplay of these two processes of intelligent activity a child assimilates new experiences to existing schemas or accommodates his schemas, by extending or combining them, to meet new situations. Consequently his schemas are highly flexible, but they maintain their property of being organized wholes although they are extended or modified. The result is that each individual becomes *adapted* to his environment by developing a sufficient repertoire of schemas to deal with the common round of events; but it is a temporary adaptation only which is modified as the environment alters or as the individual extends his range of action.

A process simultaneous with that of adaptation is *internalization* (or interiorization). Whereas the infant's world appears to be primarily one of actions and transient perceptions, an older child learns increasingly to represent the world mentally by means of memories, imagery, and language or symbols, until in adolescence thought may proceed entirely in imagination without recourse to overt actions. In young infants Piaget found no evidence of internalized thinking and, consequently, no evidence of memory as older children or adults experience it. A selection from Piaget's observations shows how memory develops and that, in the first place, it is still tied to the child's physical actions.

Obs. 2. Laurent, as early as the second day, seems to seek with his lips the breast which has escaped him. Obs. 4, 5, 8, 10. From the third day he gropes more systematically to find it. Obs. 17, 18, etc. From 0;1(2) and 0;1(3) he searches in the same way for his thumb which brushed his mouth. (Piaget, 1953a.)

In these observations we see the pursuit of objects which have disappeared, in the first case in connection with a reflex activity and with an acquired habit in the second case. Somewhat later Piaget observes:

Obs. 2. . . . Jacqueline, as early as 0;2(27) follows her

5

mother with her eyes, and when her mother leaves the visual field, continues to look in the same direction until the picture reappears. (Piaget, 1955.)
Obs. 48. From 0;1(26) . . . Laurent turns in the right direction as soon as he hears my voice (even if he has not seen me just before) and seems satisfied when he has discovered my face. . . . (Piaget, 1953a.)

Both observations reveal expectation on the part of the infants though they involve different kinds of co-ordination of action—the one between eye and movement, the other between hearing, movement and sight. When at about four months movements of eye and hand were co-ordinated the infants brought everything they touched before their eyes, showing a comparable expectation. A few months later the infants could leave a plaything for a few minutes and then return to it:

Obs. 18. At 0;8(30) Lucienne is busy scratching a powder box placed next to her on her left, but abandons that game when she sees me appear at her right. She drops the box and plays with me for a moment, babbles etc. Then she suddenly stops looking at me and turns at once to the correct position to grasp the box; obviously she does not doubt that this will be at her disposal in the very place where she used it before. (Piaget, 1955.)

But Piaget continues in explanation:

All that the child assumes is that . . . in lowering his hand he will again find the tactile impression experienced shortly before . . . ; but this return to the initial position is still determined by the activity itself, the advantage of this position rising merely from the fact that it characterized the beginning of the action in progress. Proof of this interpretation . . . is that the child makes no attempt to search for the object when it is neither within an extension of the gesture made, nor in its initial position.

So far then memory is only partly internalized, for it

depends on physical action. At the end of the period of infancy, however, a kind of memory has evolved which possibly depends on imagery and certainly requires the capacity to use symbols. For example, by about eighteen months a child may pretend to sleep or put his doll to bed. Such a schema of action is removed from its context, for it evokes an absent situation which the child recalls. Similarly he may use pebbles to symbolize sweets though he has had none for several days, and so on.

Thinking, including its memory aspects, grows gradually through the internalization of action. An infant or young child acts to achieve a result but cannot hold in mind a sequence of actions; a child of about seven or more shows that he can imagine actions. For example, the infant knows how to turn a box round to reach the other side, but an older child may be able to see in his mind's eye a series of different rotations of the block and to succeed in drawing successive views.

Development in children's thinking

In the first eighteen months, or so, of life, the infant's learning consists in developing and co-ordinating his actions and perceptions into organized *schemas of action,* or *sensori-motor schemas.* But, with ability to use symbols, a new kind of schema develops. This is the *representational schema.* Piaget's observations suggest that the capacity to use representational schemas in delayed imitation, or in playing a role, is fairly independent of the development of language, for deaf mutes too may learn this. It depends instead on a general capacity to represent one thing by another and derives from the sensori-motor schemas themselves. For example, in the case of Lucienne, 'make-belief' or 'symbolic play' made its appearance at 1;0(0), arising from a schema of action:

Obs. 65. She was sitting in her cot when she unintentionally fell backwards. Then, seeing a pillow, she got into the position for sleeping on her side. . . . She remained in this position for a moment, then sat up delightedly. During the day she went through the process again a number of times, although she was no longer in her cot; first she smiled (this indication of the representation symbol is to be noted), then threw herself back, turned on her side, put her hands over her face as if she held a pillow . . . and remained motionless, with her eyes open, smiling quietly. The symbol was therefore established. (Piaget, 1951.)

Ability to see resemblances between actions, or situations, has already been developed in the sensori-motor schemas of later infancy—in balancing different suspended objects, obtaining various objects too distant to reach by dragging their supports or through imitation of other person's actions which leads the infant to recognize similarities between himself and others. From recognition of resemblances it is a short step to *representative schemas*. Language, however, may be essential to their further development for it replaces actions, and eventually verbal thought transcends action by its speed and flexibility.

With the appearance of symbolic representation all thinking must be reconstructed on a new plane. Where an infant makes detours and reversals in action, the older child reverses an object or represents a series of rotations in thought; where the infant makes physical movements along a complex route returning to the starting-point, the boy must learn to understand an imaginary system of displacements; where the infant aimed at success in action, the older child learns to describe and consider his techniques so that he can select the most successful one in thought, or, at least, he makes a plan of action.

Immediately following the sensori-motor period there is a stage of development in which thinking, though representational, is not yet conceptual. This stage Piaget calls the *pre-conceptual* stage; the young child cannot yet under-

proximity of ideas or expressions
ii place or time as principle
of association

THE DEVELOPMENT OF INTELLIGENCE

stand how to make classes and to see their inter-relationships; he sees resemblances, between clouds and smoke
from a pipe for example, or he groups things together
from chance contiguity or because they mean something
to him. In this stage he may talk of the 'moons' when it
appears to him that he sees a succession of moons during
a journey, or he says 'the slug' as he sees a number of
slugs during a walk, as though one might be appearing in
different places. It does not interest him whether there is
one or many. His schemas still, in part, derive from his
actions—he believes that a mountain actually changes in
shape during the course of a journey he makes—but they
are also representative schemas in so far as he tries to
link a group of events or objects by a type individual.
The smoke from a pipe may be linked in his mind with
smoke from chimneys or bonfires and mist, clouds, steam
etc. His judgments derive from his own experiences; he
says 'It is wrong to tell a lie because you will be smacked.'
If he is given a collection of coloured shapes and is asked
to put together 'those that go together' he will make a
house or a train or some other construction which interests him; he does not think to classify by colour or by
shape although he perceives them. Thinking which is dis-
torted in this way to the child's point of view Piaget calls
'*egocentric*'. The egocentric thinker assimilates experiences from the world at large into schemas derived from
his own immediate world, seeing everything in relation to
himself. Consequently he attributes life and feeling, in the
first place, to all objects, though later only to those which
move; he believes that natural objects are man-made and
that they can be influenced by his wishes or by actions at
a distance; and he supposes that his dreams and thoughts
are accessible immediately to other people. He does not
see the world as consisting in natural objects which have
relations to each other, or himself as an independent object
within this world. In short, his conception of the world is
similar to that of men in many primitive societies.

9

Piaget's study of children's development in the use of language (Piaget, 1926) in which the conversations of twenty children between four and seven were recorded, and of two six-year-olds in more detail, shows that monologue plays an important role in early thinking. A close link was found between words and actions. Children uttered words to initiate actions and frequently soliloquized as they worked, apparently with no further aim than to accompany actions as they took place. In a second kind of soliloquy, speech served less to accompany or to accelerate action as to replace it by illusory achievement; the child would forget his actions and do nothing but talk, commanding animate and inanimate things. Among the two six-year-olds this happened more frequently in the one who was less well adjusted socially but who had an exuberant imagination. A different kind of monologue occurred as children talked aloud in the presence of others without waiting for, or seemingly desiring, any reply. In the case of each six-year-old over forty per cent of his speech was of these kinds. Again, since it referred to the child's own actions, Piaget termed this 'egocentric' speech. The rest of the children's conversation consisted in social speech : giving information, asking and answering questions, argument by means of clashing affirmations, criticism and derision, commands, requests and threats.

Towards the end of the pre-conceptual stage children's pre-conceptual thinking develops to a point at which they are capable of giving reasons for their beliefs. Where a younger child asked why he thinks a motor-car is alive replies 'Because I do', the child at the end of this stage may reply 'Because it goes fast'. His thinking remains egocentric but he attains some true concepts; that is to say he can classify objects correctly, or possibly, can put them in order of size. If he is asked to sort coloured shapes into 'those which go together' he will now arrange them in lines by colour or by shape, though it will not occur to him to arrange them simultaneously according to both classifications. Indeed he has difficulty in dealing with two relations at a time. If, when he has made two equal lines of counters, one is removed he believes that the numbers of counters are no longer equal; he cannot take account both of number and length of line. He supposes that water poured from a short, broad glass into a tall, thin one changes in quantity, for although he can describe the glasses he cannot see how the dimensions compensate each other. The difficulty is evident also when a child is asked about the relations between a whole and its parts, or between a class and its sub-classes. An interesting experiment of André Rey (1950) displays that their difficulty is a mental one. He drew a square, with side a few centimetres, on a large square piece of paper and asked people of different ages to draw the smallest and largest squares possible on the same page. Adults and children over about 7-8 years immediately drew a very tiny square and one following the edge of the paper. But children in the intuitive stage at first drew squares little smaller or larger than the standard, proceeding from these by successive drawings (often unsuccessful) to still smaller or larger ones, evidently unable to anticipate the final result without first seeing and making a series of squares. Since the action was not yet *internalized* they could not form the mental actions or operations leading to the result. Lacking a mental structure to enable them to make comparisons, children at this stage make judgments on the basis of perception : so a line of counters is either more or less in number than another according to how it is spread out or pushed together; journeys take equal times if their end points are level, without regard to actual length of journey or times of arrival and departure. Piaget calls this stage in thinking the *intuitive stage*. In intuitive thinking, which depends on perceptual judgments, conclusions may differ. Consequently such thinking is not 'reversible' in the way that logical thinking is. A logical operation is reversible. If, for example, we add three to two we obtain five; if we now reverse the operation and subtract three we are back to where we began. It will always be so whoever makes the experiment, wherever it is made. But if judgments are made perceptually they differ from person to person or in the same person on different occasions.

Gradually as a result of their actions children internalize ideas of classes and series. When this occurs they have reached the *period of concrete operations*. They are able to explain classes they have made and to understand relationships between them. But it is not a total departure from the active world of younger children, for Piaget considers that the action in reality is replaced by an action in imagination, called an *operation*, which may depend on imagery at least in the first place. However, operations are imagined actions which are no longer tied to physical possibilities or limited and confused by 'centring' on one aspect or another; a child can now imagine the same liquid in either of two containers, or the same beads in either of two necklaces or as members of either of two classes, and so on.

In mathematics and science, much thinking consists in mental actions which are symbolized by various signs and figures. To take an example given by Piaget:

In any expression, such as $(x^2+y=z-u)$, each term refers to a specific action: the sign $=$ expresses a possible substitution, the sign $(+)$ a combination, the sign $(-)$ a separation, the sign (x^2) the action of reproducing 'x' x times, and each of the values u, x, y and z the action of reproducing unity a certain number of times So each of these symbols refers to an action which could be realized, but which mathematical language contents itself with describing in the form of internalized actions i.e. operations of thought. (Piaget, 1950.)

When logical thinking is attained a further development may occur in passing from *concrete operations* to the more abstract *formal operations*. Concrete operations are logical operations, such as classifications, seriations, symmetry, one-one or one-many correspondences, and so on; but their use is limited to actual objects or materials or to ones which can easily be imagined. The algebraic operations just cited would be difficult to the child in the period of concrete operations unless they could be represented in some solid or visual form—as they might be with the Dienes apparatus; but this, of course, confines the question to the particular case being illustrated. It is the adolescent who can see the general meaning of 'the variable x'; he no longer needs to deal directly with objects but can use verbal elements alone. In addition, where the child deals logically with single relations the adolescent can structure relations between relations as in proportionality; for he can make a relation between two comparisons, where the child makes a single comparison, or single equation, only. But possibly the most distinctive differences in thinking are firstly, that in a problem situation the child proceeds by trial and error until he hits on a right solution as a result of his action, whereas the adolescent mentally makes plans of action based on hypotheses which he proceeds to test. He argues, 'If it were (such and such a factor) then (such and such) a consequence would follow.' Thus he attains hypothetico-deductive thinking. Secondly, within his environment he seeks all-embracing causes or explanations and general laws where the child merely describes or is content with partial explanations.

Before proceeding to outline the main periods of cognitive development it remains to mention influences on cognition other than the child's own actions. These are largely concerned with the opportunities afforded by his environment. For example, Africans who have few opportunities to use manual skills develop spatial concepts later and less accurately than do English children; and the language of a tribe may lack words for certain concepts and so inhibit their development. Children from poor social backgrounds whose parents rarely talk to them and who use their vocabulary inaccurately are at a disadvantage in all verbal skills. Piaget's description of the adaptation of the individual to his environment would lead us to expect such results, but he does not usually stress the importance of the nature of their environment in discussing observations or experiments with children, nor has he attempted to discover the possible extent of individual differences in ability; he suggests only that able or backward children may reach each stage sooner or later than average ones. And he has not considered the possible effects of individuals favouring different ways of perceiving the world, whether these arise from early choices, disabilities, or differences in innate capacities; yet such differences must have an effect on the organization of mental structures. We shall see in citing references at the ends of later chapters that the stage of mental development is more closely correlated with mental than with chronological age; and it must suffice to mention the work of M. D. Vernon (1962) to show that individuals may favour different kinds of perceptual and intellectual procedures. Piaget also almost entirely neglects affective influences on thinking; but, as we shall see in discussion at the ends of later chapters, in particular Chapter 2, affective components enter into every cognitive structure. Severe emotional deprivation may drastically limit intellectual development, and, as everyone knows from experience, distaste for certain studies with some limitation in these areas, follows on unpleasant or uncongenial experiences in learning.

So many possible influences on the level of thinking attained result inevitably in uneven development, as we see if we test any one child in a wide range of concepts. Although much of his thinking may be at the level of concrete operations he may regress to intuitive or preconceptual thinking in unfamiliar fields of knowledge, or even if unfamiliar materials are introduced in testing. Regression is commonly observed also in cases of emotional disturbance. On the other hand special experiences, which include those he has in school, may enable him to think at the level of formal operations in some limited field or in easier and more familiar situations. Consequently the clear-cut periods of development which we are about to outline, though a useful guide, do not accurately represent mental development for individuals.

The main periods of development

Piaget and his chief collaborator, Inhelder, believe that they can distinguish three main periods in which cognitive development is qualitatively different, with sub-stages in each. The first of these is the *period of sensori-motor intelligence* which extends from birth until the appearance of language, approximately during the first eighteen months of life. The second period extends from this time until about eleven or twelve years and consists in preparation for, and realization of, *concrete operations of classes, relations and numbers*. The third period, that of *formal operations*, begins at about twelve years and achieves its full development roughly three years later. The second period they subdivide. Period IIA extends from about eighteen months to about seven years, and is a pre-operational period. It is again subdivided into two stages; the first extending until about four years they call the *pre-conceptual stage*; the second is the *intuitive stage*. Period IIB extends roughly from seven years to adolescence and is the *period of concrete operations*.

Most of the child's thinking in any one stage or period has a characteristic structure. In period I it is a system of 'reversible' actions, where by 'reversible' Piaget means that the child can retrace his action by successive movements. In period IIA (i) and (ii) the structures are representative but are not operational or reversible. In period IIB the concrete operations are logical operations which, as we shall see at the end of Chapter 5, all obey the same five laws of 'groupings'. Finally, the more complex and abstract hypothetico-deductive thinking of the adolescent is subject to the mathematical laws of the groups and the lattice.

As children develop, the structure built at a younger age evolves gradually into an integral part of the structure of the following stage. For example, the idea that an object is a permanent thing, which is learned gradually in the first period, is necessary to the notion of conservation of quantity which is learned in the period of concrete operations. Similarly concrete operations form a basis for the system of formal operations which succeed them; to understand proportionality in adolescence, the child must first learn to compare any two quantitives or to equalize them, as he does in the period of concrete operations.

It follows that the order of the periods of development is constant; one structure cannot appear before another in a certain number of children and after it with another group of children. But the age at which a stage is realized cannot be absolutely fixed, for it is always relative to the environment which may encourage, impede or even prevent its appearance. In addition, a stage may appear fairly early with one kind of situation or material but later with another. The children tested by Piaget and his collaborators understood that substance was conserved, when shape was altered at about six years, but conservation of volume was not understood until about ten or eleven years. When the same operation is applied to different content at different ages Piaget speaks of *horizontal displacement*.

A second kind of 'displacement' in which a structure is reconstructed by means of different operations he calls a *'vertical displacement'*. For example, the baby in the sensori-motor period can orient himself in his environment by movements, turning himself and returning to his original position; several years later he can represent these same displacements mentally—the operation has become internalized. In this case the same situation is dealt with at a different level of mental organization.

Experiments in England

Experiments, similar to those of Piaget, in England appear to confirm, at least roughly, the existence of his major periods of development. Recent experiments under the direction of Professor Peel at Birmingham University confirm that formal operations do not appear, in general, until adolescence. But their appearance is related more closely with mental age than with chronological age. An investigation into problem-solving in science among adolescents in a comprehensive school made by Mealings (1963) suggests that a mental age of at least thirteen is required before boys and girls structure relations between relations or can make use of proportionality, and that more usually a mental age of fifteen or sixteen must be reached before thinking at the level of formal operations can be expected. However, we have only to consider the vast differences in thinking between men in primitive societies and those in industrial ones to realize that these developments are to a large extent socially and educationally determined.

2

The sensori-motor period

The sensori-motor period, as we have seen, is the period of mental development which begins with capacity for a few reflexes, and ends when language and other symbolic ways of representing the world first appear. Since the achievements of this period underlie all further cognitive advances, it is of fundamental importance. It may be that children's development during this period differs less than at any subsequent period for, in infancy, differences in the use of language are of little importance, and other differences in environment must amount to the extremes of neglect or physical handicap before they seriously limit an infant's capacity to enlarge his range of action or to co-ordinate his actions and perceptions. Consequently, the mental development of Piaget's three children on which his conclusions are based may be fairly typical for infants in general, except in so far as their innate capacities differed from those of other children.

In a number of books Piaget has described the gradual development of memory as we know it, changes in imitation and play, and acquisition of the first notions of conservation of the object, and of space, time and physical causality. The children's development is considered in each of these fields separately, using many observations in illustration. Since in this volume brevity is important, we

18

shall consider the developments in each sub-stage of the period, mentioning different kinds of development as they are relevant.

Sub-stages i and ii. Reflex exercises and primary circular reactions

Piaget observed that the tendency to repeat reflex actions and to assimilate new objects into them appeared within less than one hour of birth in two of his children. Lucienne and Laurent had already sucked their hands within fifteen and thirty minutes of birth. When not engaged in sucking to obtain food all three children sucked anything which came in contact with their lips and learned very quickly to relinquish unsatisfactory objects, such as the blanket. Similarly, their hands were constantly in action, grasping what came in contact with them, while a cousin at six days already directed his eyes towards the light. Within the first month, which is roughly the duration of stage (i), an assortment of such schemas of action had been built up.

In stage (ii) the new ability to follow objects with their eyes allows the infants to explore their surroundings (Obs. 28. Piaget, 1953a). For the first time, at 24 days, Jacqueline lay awake without crying, gazing at objects ahead of her. It was at this stage that new activities appeared which were not directly derived from reflexes; the infants began to co-ordinate movements of the arm and mouth, for example, enabling them to suck their thumbs at will. Piaget calls such activities the *first acquired adaptations*. Vision and hearing were also co-ordinated, but Piaget observed of Laurent that he did not attempt to look for the owner of a voice unless he had seen the face beforehand in motion. Successful cycles of action, of this kind, Piaget calls the *primary circular reactions*. In Piaget's view their existence is evidence of the dawning of memory and causality and, since the order of actions is important, some

Actually
with two
2-3 wks old

sense of a time sequence is implied. But, although there is a beginning to co-ordination, each perceptual 'bundle' tends to remain a separate 'space' : there are still unrelated groups of actions which are centred on the mouth, the hands, the eyes or on movements of the limbs, each proceeding independently.

In discussing the development of ideas of space, Piaget uses the concept of *groups* of displacements or transpositions. Actions or operations of displacement form a group so soon as the infant shows a practical appreciation of how to co-ordinate them to achieve some desired end—as in thumb-sucking, for instance. It is a characteristic of a group of displacements that they are *reversible*, that is to say they can be reversed to bring them back to the initial point. The main practical groups which follow from the capacity for visual accommodation occur in following movements of translation, in finding the position of objects and in estimating distances in depth. But, in the first two stages groups of displacements are 'practical groups' achieved entirely by motor co-ordination without giving rise to mental representation.

Imitation during this stage goes beyond the sympathetic crying of stage (i) to include imitation of actions which the child has already discovered for himself, such as head nodding and hand clasping. Laurent (Obs. 74 Piaget, 1953a) imitated his father's clasped hands when these were at a distance of twenty to thirty centimetres from his eyes but grasped them if they were close enough. Piaget suggested that the latter response might be due to an assimilation to the child's visual image of his own hands clasping.

Circular reactions were imposed on reflex phonation as soon as one or two months. The little wails which preceded crying were kept up for their own sake, gradually giving rise to modulations. In such actions and in the repetition of physical actions accompanied by smiling we may see the beginning of games, but, as yet, they are not differentiated from the infant's other activities.

20

Sub-stage iii. The secondary circular reactions

Whereas primary circular reactions are actions repeated for their own sakes without attempts to use them to an end, *secondary circular reactions* are movements centred on a result produced in the external environment with the sole aim of maintaining it. When given a new toy the infant uses it to try out all his schemas of action but, if a satisfying result is obtained, he attempts to reproduce it.

> Obs. 110. At 0;3(29) for the first time Laurent sees the paper-knife. He grasps it and looks at it, but only for a moment. Afterwards he immediately swings it with his right hand as he does all objects he grasps. He then rubs it by chance against the wicker of the bassinet and tries to reproduce the sound heard, as though it were a rattle. . . .
>
> at 0;6(16) a new swan, encircled by a ring and with a handle, is looked at with curiosity and immediately shaken, struck, rubbed, etc. (Piaget, 1955.)

Co-ordination of eye and hand which usually develops in the fourth month enables the children to extend the range of their actions.

> Obs. 102. Laurent, at 0;3(6) grasps a rattle after seeing his hand in the same visual field, then brings it to his mouth. At 0;4(28) Obs. 103, Lucienne attempts to grasp the rattle which is attached to the hood of the pram. (Piaget, 1953a.)

An element of *foresight* of events thus appears for the first time: the string hanging from the pram hood is not only to be seen, grasped and pulled, but it serves to swing objects from a distance, etc. Foresight is also evident in relation to sounds and actions; for example:

> Obs. 108. From 0;4(12) to approximately 0;4(30) Laurent cried with rage when, after his feedings, a handkerchief

or napkin was placed under his chin; they announced a few spoonfuls of a beverage he disliked. At 0;7(10) he cried in the morning as soon as he heard his mother's bed creak. Until then, although awake he did not show his hunger. (ibid.)

Imitation becomes more deliberate and systematic. All three infants imitated any gesture known to them with the exception of gestures they could not see themselves make.

Notions of the object, space, time and physical causality

Unfamiliar objects provoke little surprise but objects are now recognized as having certain permanent properties although the recognition is limited by the extent of the infant's actions. At first at about five months there is no reaction to a falling object if it is outside the cot or pram except to look at the hands which dropped it, but the infants react by looking at the coverlet when an object is dropped onto it. But two months later, when sitting on the floor, the children will look on the floor for objects dropped above them provided they had glimpsed the beginning of the movement. Also at the beginning of the stage the permanence of objects is recognized in so far that the infants search with their hands for objects which they have let go; but at six months Laurent seems to believe that the object has disappeared if he does not find it by lowering his arm for he does not search the surrounding area if he fails to find it at once (Obs. 17. Piaget, 1955). Nor is the permanence of the object recognized when only part of it is seen.

Their notions of causality show similar limitations. The children use actions of striking, arching themselves, pulling etc. to produce the continuation of unconnected events.

Obs. 112. 0;7(2) Laurent is in the process of striking a cushion, when I snap my middle finger against the ball of my thumb. Laurent then smiles and strikes the cushion but while staring at my hand; as I no longer move he strikes harder and harder and with a definite expression of desire and expectation and, at the moment when I resume snapping my fingers, he stops as though he had achieved his object. (Piaget, 1953a.)

However, although schemas which are successful in some situations are used indiscriminately the child begins to examine successful actions; for example, he makes his hand perform all sorts of actions which he examines attentively. Sometimes this appears to be for the sake of imitation or to evaluate distances or to construct his space in depth—but there is some appreciation of causality unconnected with the child's immediate actions in searching for the causes of unexpected events and perceptions.

In the spatial field groups of displacements transcend the purely practical groups of the previous stages in so far as the infant tries to watch what he is doing, so arriving at an elementary perception of the group. But, as we have seen in his reactions to objects, space remains limited by the child's field of action and therefore cannot yet consist in a system of relationships between objects but is only an aggregate of relations; perceived practically and centred on the child himself. However, since groups of actions are interco-ordinated under the influence of prehension, and since the child begins to observe his actions, Piaget distinguishes them from the purely practical groups and names them 'subjective groups'.

Since there is no true exploration of objects at this stage, ability to effect reversals, rotations and transformations remains incomplete.

Obs. 77. At 0;6(6) Laurent turns a rattle over and over, without looking at it, until he can suck the handle; . . . But in trying to steer the handle to his mouth he catches it on his arm (he sees this happen); he pulls harder and harder but does not succeed in correcting the movement by turning the rattle in the other direction. (Piaget, 1955.)

A month later Laurent is able to turn his bottle about, is allowed to view both ends but, presented with the wrong end, sucks it, looks at it, sucks again and becomes discouraged. He must see some of the rubber before he realizes that he should turn the bottle round.

An interesting limitation of the period, both spatially and temporally is that the infant looks back to the place where an event first occurred in the hope of seeing it again despite subsequent events:

> Obs. 171. 0;8(7). His mother having risen and left the room, Laurent watches her until she reaches the door, then, as soon as she disappears, again looks for her behind him in the place where she was at first. (Piaget, 1955.)

Sub-stage iv. Co-ordination of secondary schemas

The essential novelty in this stage is that the child no longer only tries to repeat or prolong an effect which he had discovered or observed by chance but pursues an end not immediately attainable and tries to reach it by different intermediate means. An example, one of many, serves to show the nature of this development.

> Obs. 121. At 0;8(20) Jacqueline tries to grasp a cigarette case I present to her. I then slide it between the crossed strings which attach her dolls to the hood. She tries to reach it directly. Not succeeding, she immediately looks for the strings which are not in her hands and of which she saw only the part in which the cigarette case is entangled. She looks in front of her, grasps the strings, pulls and shakes them etc. The cigarette case then falls and she grasps it. (Piaget, 1953a.)

In Piaget's terms she has put two objects into a relationship by fusing or assimilating their schemas to each other.

24

One schema (that of pulling strings) is now included in the other (grasping an object) so that a combined schema, 'pulling strings in order to grasp', has come into being or will do so if the action is repeated.

New experiences are more fully explored than in the previous stage. Whereas in the third stage the infants tried all their schemas on each new object, in the fourth they use chance discoveries to explore actions performed on them:

Obs. 140. Laurent at 0;10(2) in examining a case of shaving soap dropped it because it was hard and slippery. Struck by this phenomenon he attempted to reproduce it, exploring the new action of 'letting go'— 'sometimes delicately opening his hand so that the case rolled along his fingers, sometimes turning his hand so that the case fell between his thumb and index finger, sometimes simply opening his hand so that the object fell'. However, he did not study the trajectory of the object but was interested solely in his own new action; so this new schema, in turn, became a means to an end. (Piaget, 1955.)

It is as a result of such exploration that schemas become 'mobile', interco-ordinating in various ways to achieve different ends, or they may again dissociate to regroup in new combinations.

New 'signs' now enable the child to foresee not only an event connected with his action, but also an independent event connected with the 'activity' of an object. Jacqueline at 0;9(16) (Obs. 133. Piaget, 1953a) recognizes the difference between the sound of a glass which contains the fruit juice she likes, and that of a bowl which contains a disliked soup. When the spoon comes from a glass she opens her mouth wide, but if from the bowl her mouth remains closed.

Such signs also assist in imitating actions with parts of the body which the child cannot see.

At 0;10(7) Obs. 135. Laurent has not succeeded in imitating the act of sticking out the tongue. Now he sticks it out spontaneously while accompanying this movement with a sound of saliva. I then imitate him and he in turn imitates me. But the imitation fails when I stick my tongue out in silence. The sound of saliva has consequently served as a sign to permit him to identify his tongue by mine. (Piaget, 1953a.)

In addition, the infants imitate visual and auditory actions which were not already familiar to them, and extend, or otherwise alter familiar actions.

(Obs. 131. Piaget, 1953a.) At 0;9(4) Laurent imitates sounds with approximately the right number of syllables saying pa for pa, papa for papa, but papapa for four or more syllables. (Obs. 25. Piaget, 1951.) Jacqueline imitates actions of putting a finger on the mouth, yawning, rubbing her eyes, sniffing, or opening and closing her eyes, showing that she had established a correspondence between parts of other faces and her own.

Games are still hardly distinct from exploration of the infants' world, but he now amuses himself by putting things in a box, removing them and repeating the action, by dropping objects and finding them again, by jerking his doll or shaking his rattle etc.

Notions of the object, space, time and physical casuality

In the field of conceptual development relating to the object, spatial understanding, and concepts of time and causality there are distinct developments. The infants now search for vanished objects, though they fail to take account of visible displacements:

Obs, 47 at 0;11(21), Jacqueline retrieves a celluloid swan hidden to her right, then to the left, but although she watches it drop, if she fails to see its final position she seeks it again where it was first hidden on her left. (Piaget, 1955.)

26

Evidently she conceives the object only in a special position—that in which it was first hidden. A residual reaction of this kind is found in much older children in relation to people.

Obs. 51 at 2;4(3), Lucienne, hearing a noise in my office, says to me (we are together in the garden), 'That is papa up there.' (Piaget, 1955.)

In dealing with spatial relationships the child for the first time appears to achieve objective groups of displacements.

Obs. 85. At 0;11(3), Lucienne hides her feet under a coverlet, then raises the coverlet, looks at them, hides them again, etc. This is a reversible group of actions, coordinated to achieve a desired end, and returning to the initial point. Similarly, in an experiment an object may pass from a child's hand to that of an observer, behind a screen, and back to the child's hand. However, the group remains elementary for the child for he cannot extend it to a succession of displacements. But, there is evidence that he begins to study the effect of displacements.

Obs. 86. Lucienne at 0;10(7) and the days following, slowly brings her face close to objects she holds until her nose is pressed against them. Then she moves away from them, looking at them very attentively, and begins over and over again. Similar observations were made, at about the same age, in the other infants. (Piaget, 1955.)

'These behaviour patterns,' says Piaget, 'which also belong to the group of reversible operations (moving forward and backward) are easy to interpret: the child is studying (by exploration . . .) this fundamental fact that an object whose tactile dimensions are constant, varies in visual shape and size according to whether it is moved towards or away from his face.' Whereas at an earlier stage he

27

might suppose that his action modified the size of the object; at this stage there is evidence that he recognizes the constancy of objects and explores the relationships of their parts. He also appears to make his first experiments with perspective, observing changes in shape as he moves his head.

> During the fourth stage the child ceases to consider his own actions as the sole source of causality and attributes to someone else's body an aggregate of particular powers. He uses someone else's body as intermediary, not as upon inert matter merely extending his own action, but by prompting the activity of the other body through a discreet pressure, a mere touch, etc.

Thus someone else's body is now regarded as an autonomous centre of causal activity and he appreciates the spatial arrangement necessary for successful action—he takes the adult's hand, putting it in the required position, for example.

Understanding of temporal sequences also increases during this stage—the infant begins to recall a sequence of ordered events, instead of recalling his actions only; but memory of actions still dominates that of displacements as in the case of the absent-minded adult who looks for a mislaid object in its usual place after putting it down in front of him.

Sub-stage v. Tertiary circular reactions

The development which occurs in the fifth stage is that an infant actively seeks new results and, having found them, accommodates to his environment by 'experimenting in order to see'. Once discovered, a new activity is reproduced so that the initial experiment is immediately accompanied by circular reactions. But these circular reactions also have a new form for they are not exact repetitions; the child repeats, but also varies, the actions which led to the new and interesting result.

For example, Obs. 141. Laurent at 0;10(10) finds a piece of bread, breaks off fragments and lets them drop, paying great attention to them in motion (whereas in stage (iv) his interest was in merely letting go of an object). The following day 'he grasps a succession of objects: a celluloid swan, a box, etc., stretches out his arm and lets them fall. He distinctly varies the position of the fall. Sometimes he stretches out his arm vertically, sometimes he holds it obliquely, in front of or behind his eyes etc. When the object falls in a new position (for example on his pillow), he lets it fall two or three times more in the same place as though to study the spatial relation; then he modifies the situation.' (Piaget, 1953a.)

In this stage, for the first time, the infant becomes capable of solving new problems even if he has no schemas immediately available to cope with them; in other words he accommodates to new situations. Piaget explains the advent of intentional accommodation by the discoveries the infants make during their efforts to assimilate new objects to their schemas in the earlier stages; in this way they discover the resistance of certain objects and the existence of properties irreducible to existing schemas. As a result accommodation acquires an interest in itself and, although the infant may experiment blindly at first, his activities are soon guided by previous learning for he assimilates new discoveries as they occur.

The first manifestation of inventive intelligence observed in Piaget's three children was to draw distant objects closer by means of something beneath them, for example a cushion to obtain a box lying on it. If this response occurred by chance in the fourth stage it did not result in learning, but at the fifth stage experiments 'in order to see' had resulted in a fund of experiences in which similarities were observed; so Jacqueline, for example, knew that she could act on objects by means of intermediaries and draw her duck to her by pulling the coverlet. In another

29

observation we see Lucienne at 1;1(3) learning to put a long chain in a pail so that the weight of the protruding end is not great enough to remove it again. (Obs. 171-173, Piaget, 1953a.) In every case there is a goal to be achieved, some groping co-ordination of schemas and production of new schemas. There is also the beginning of recognition that objects may cause phenomena independent of the child's action; at 1;3(12) Jacqueline carefully approaches and very cautiously collects her clown from the top of the playpen because she knows that it will fall at the slightest shake.

In stage (v) the children proceed with great perseverance and assurance, groping to a perfect imitation of an unfamiliar action. In play, they repeat actions, such as series of 'ritual gestures', for example, and use noises repetitively in play, repeat movements required in balancing, but also introduce variations into their games.

Notions of the object, space, time and physical causality

Developments of 'concepts' of object, space, time and causality follow from experimentation. All three infants learned to take account of sequential movements of objects, though they could keep track only of displacements they observed. The object acquired a real permanence and a physical identity independent of its movements in the field of prehension or in depth.

The children recognized the need for contacts and intermediaries between themselves and objects on which they wished to act and allowed for systems of causes independent of their own actions, such as the action of gravity on falling or sliding objects, the independent actions of other persons, and so on. At this stage, instead of attempting to induce their parents' co-operation by moving themselves they placed a box they wanted opened into the parental hand, put themselves in position ready for the parent to continue to play a game etc. Also spatial relations were taken into account; for example, Lucienne at 1;0(5) turns a box to get at an object on its far side, evidently having established a causal and spatial relation between support and object. (Obs. 152. Piaget, 1953a.)

Some games appear to have the purpose of elaborating spatial groups.

> Obs. 104a. At 1;1(18) Lucienne is seated on the ground; she puts a doll behind her with one hand and takes it with the other, turning to the opposite side. At 1;3(17) she drops a shoe behind her head over her shoulders, then turns, finds it and begins again. They apply them equally to other persons; Piaget reports in the same observations of Laurent at 1;2(26) . . . 'I put a spoon behind me; he immediately goes round me and finds it.' (Piaget, 1955.)

Other observations show interest in equilibrium and position. There is also an interest in the relation of contents to container; at the beginning of the second year all three children begin to put solid objects into hollow ones and to empty the latter by turning them upside-down. There is evidence too of study of rotations and reversals in playing with toys: opening a watch, folding material, etc. On the whole the child succeeds in making objective spatial groups in every domain but these groups are limited to spatial displacements actually seen and cannot yet be extended to any imagined displacement. In other words, the child does not yet know either how to take account of displacements produced outside his perceptual field or how to picture himself as a moving object in the environment.

The organization of spatial groups in this stage also give rise to appreciation of an ordered sequence of events, to some conception of 'before' and 'after' and a more prolonged memory for a sequence of displacements. But when actions are too far separated in time and thus require an exact representative memory to be arranged in order, the child relapses into his earlier difficulties.

Sub-stage vi. The invention of new means through mental combinations

In the sixth stage the child begins to invent as well as to discover; he begins to replace sensori-motor groping by mental combinations giving him an immediate solution to problems; that is to say, he begins to be able to represent the external world mentally in images, memories and symbols which he can combine without making further physical actions. At first sight it might seem that these mental structures organize themselves and are totally different in kind from the empirical gropings of the preceding stage, but in Piaget's view both derive equally from the complementary processes of assimilation and accommodation, differing only in speed. As we have seen, in discussing the fifth stage, there is no pure accommodation for it is always directed by schemas already known to the child, and as they are modified by new discoveries. While the child has much to discover, the structuring goes on at a slow pace; but in the sixth stage his mind is already well furnished with schemas which can be reorganized spontaneously as a result of his many experiments in the fifth stage. Piaget finds that invention is no more than this rapid organization and that representation amounts to the power to evoke well-known schemas mentally. For example:

Obs. 180. At 1;4(0) Lucienne proves able to extract a chain from a match-box if it is given to her with an opening of 10 mm., for she puts in her fingers, extracts a small piece of chain and pulls out the rest. But when the opening is only 3 mm. this method fails. 'She looks at the slit with great attention; then, several times in succession she opens and shuts her mouth, at first slightly, then wider and wider! . . . Lucienne by opening her mouth thus expresses, or even reflects, her desire to enlarge the opening of the box. This schema of imitation, with which she is familiar, constitutes for her the means of thinking out the situation. . . . Soon after this phase of plastic reflection, Lucienne unhesitatingly puts her finger in the slit, and, instead of trying as before to reach the chain, she pulls so as to enlarge the opening. She succeeds and grasps the chain.' (Piaget, 1955.)

Since she has no words or clear visual images with which to symbolize the experiment, she uses a simple motor indication as a symbol and performs it beforehand instead of groping for a solution with the object.

In Jacqueline at 1;8(30), a sudden discovery that she must turn over a brown pencil, as she has done a green one, to insert its point in a hole (Obs. 182. Piaget, 1955), shows an instant mental assimilation to a previously successful schema without progressive gropings in action. In a new situation the already acquired schemas direct the search at the moment of invention, although no one of them may in itself contain the correct solution. Lucienne has already played with a chain, rolling it up, or inserting it in a wide opening and has compared large objects to inadequate openings, making apertures wider, consequently it remains only to assimilate these schemas reciprocally to each other to arrive at a solution.

As yet the infants do not think in terms of images, but use images or some transitional symbolic action as occasional aids in thinking. In the example we have quoted Lucienne used a kind of imitation. Imitation of movements which he cannot see himself make, lead to representation of his own face, whereas delayed imitation (of absent persons, for example) precedes symbolism. Play also becomes symbolic, for the infants now pretend to perform actions or make their toys do so. In addition, 'deferred imitation' appears; such as imitating an absent sister's behaviour, and this is more remarkable as the child is imitating for the first time in the absence of a model. Piaget suggests that the mental image (i.e. the symbol when it is the interior copy of reproduction of the object) is merely the product of the interiorization of imitation. ['When the

33

accommodation of sensori-motor schemas takes the form of visible gestures, it constitutes imitation proper, but when, sufficiently developed to need no external experiment, it remains virtual and interior, would it not lead to interiorized imitation which is the image?'] . . . The line of development of the mental image in the sixth stage is similar to the development of the interiorization of language in the child of 2 to 4 or 5 years, but language is much more socialized than the image.

In the development of conceptual thinking also the new capacity for mental representation plays an important part. A child who realizes that objects are permanent can find them when displacements invisible to him have occurred, even after several sequential displacements. For example,

Obs. 123. At 1:6(8) Jacqueline throws a ball under a sofa . . . she looks at the place, realizes that the ball must have crossed under the sofa and sets out to go behind it.

Obs. 125. Laurent at 1;3(4) made a detour round a wall to open a gate from the other side.

Obs. 126. Jacqueline at 1;11(10) can point back at the house on the way home; though she begins by pointing behind her, she changes her mind when she realizes that they are on the return trip. (Piaget, 1955.)

Likewise the children seek causes which they have not perceived:

Obs. 156. Jacqueline is examining the arm of an old armchair, unfamiliar to her, with an extension leaf used for trays, which I operate from behind. This time Jacqueline has not seen me do this, and does not see my arm when I push the leaf. Nevertheless when it slips Jacqueline immediately turns to me, looks at my hand and definitely shows by her behaviour that she considers me the cause of the object's movement. (Piaget, 1955.)

Obs. 159. Laurent at only 1;4(4) looks for and removes an obstruction when he cannot open a door. (ibid.)

But in new situations, or in one hard to understand, the children attempt to use actions at a distance to achieve their ends: blinking to make a light come on, striking a chair as though this will make the windows open wider, or using actions of their own as though these will directly cause some action on the part of an adult.

Mental representation extends time to more than the immediate past.

Obs. 173. At 1;7(25) Jacqueline is reminded by a blade of grass of the grasshoppers she saw a few days before and speaks of them. She can point correctly in the direction of a journey her grandfather had taken two days before and recalls a conversation after a lapse of two days. (Obs. 173a, ibid.)

However, the sequence of events remembered are isolated; there is nothing here which will enable the child to reconstruct his own history or to consider his acts as succeeding one another.

But at the end of the period the child's own body is regarded as an object. Thanks to imitation . . . the child is now able to see his own body as an object by analogy with that of another person. Moreover, nascent spatial, temporal and causal images permit him to locate himself in a space and time reaching beyond him everywhere, and to consider himself a mere cause and mere effect among the totality of the connections he discovers. His world has become a solid universe of co-ordinated objects including the body itself in the capacity of an element. (Piaget, 1955.)

Discussion

The reader may question whether every infant passes through the six stages outlined by Piaget and at the same time other psychologists who have studied infants' development have reported wide ranges of ages at which skills or abilities have developed (Bayley, 1933). However, there is the difference that Piaget is not so much concerned with particular abilities, such as capacity to balance one thing or another, for instance, as with the infants' methods of responding to their environment or organizing their experiences. Piaget's sample of infants was very small since it consisted of his own three children whose genetic constitutions and environments would necessarily be rather similar. To determine whether or not these stages are of general use in describing developments, many more observations and experiments are needed of infants from a wide range of backgrounds during the first two years of life. A few observations made by students in Birmingham in the early 1960s showed that several English infants reached the stages described by Piaget somewhat earlier than his children did in the 1930s, but this could well be due to differences in infant care.

What Piaget has drawn our attention to is the importance of each infant's activities and his ability to organize them in relation to opportunities afforded within his environment. It follows that an infant from a stimulating environment surrounded by adults or other children who play with him, enriching his experiences and helping him to organize them, will be in advance of infants whose environment is less stimulating and who receive inadequate care. There is already an accumulation of evidence that the development of infants can be seriously retarded in an environment in which they receive little attention or affection. The reader is referred to Anastasi (1958) for extensive accounts of such investigations as we can mention only a few such studies here. For example, Goldfarb (1955) compared young children brought up in institutions from birth with those who entered at three years old and found that the latter group had a mean I.Q. of 95·4, but those who had always been in institutions had a mean I.Q. of only

72·4. With still less adequate adult contact than that afforded in these American institutions of the early 1950s, both physical and personality development are very considerably delayed; children show resistance to new situations, become depressed and withdrawn, show extreme retardation in behaviour development as well as incapacity to learn and have increased susceptibility to disease (Spitz, 1945). Perhaps in the long run the most serious result of severe deprivation in infancy is that when infants become adults they tend to make inadequate parents who repeat with their own offspring the treatment meted out to them. Studies of rhesus monkeys brought up in an environment lacking a comforting mother figure or companionship show both the incapacity to play normally during 'childhood' and inability to become adequate parents to the next generation (Harlow, 1959). Among human beings subsequent experiences may modify the effects of even the most extremely limited home environment but there are, nevertheless, children and adults whose behaviour parallels that of the deprived rhesus monkeys. Less extreme emotional deprivation, as Goldfarb showed, is likely to limit development of the higher mental capacities.

There is no similar body of investigations into the effects of enriching the environment of infants; but, what little evidence there is suggests, as we would expect, that it can have lasting consequences. For example, only children and, to a lesser extent, eldest children are on the average, more advanced in development of speech and vocabulary than children of multiple births or of young siblings (Davis, 1937). Probably the undivided attention of an adult and the greater opportunities they have for conversation with adults gives them a lasting advantage. There is also a preponderance of eldest sons among distinguished scientists (Ellis, 1904). Similarly, in an environment in which several languages are spoken one sees that infants already pick up the variety of sounds without difficulty and may retain the skill in making them even if they speak only one of the languages during childhood. It is likely also that the many mechanical and constructional toys for infants in industrial societies give them an advantage in developing mechanical skills in later life. In communities which neither provide mechanical toys nor allow children to participate in the adults' constructional activities the children tend to be much slower in developing mechanical and spatial understanding (Beard, 1968 and McFie, 1961); but this, of course, is a cumulative effect due to fewer experiences of these kinds throughout childhood. Experiments with animals tend to confirm these findings: the chimpanzee, Viki, who was reared with a child achieved all the non-verbal skills normal in a child of her age when she was six, and rats and dogs reared in a rich perceptual environment, when compared with those from less stimulating surroundings, learned more quickly and solved problems more successfully when adult (Forgus, 1954 and Hayes and Hayes, 1951).

Thus both Piaget's investigations and those of other psychologists lead one to conclude that the provision of a stimulating environment together with considerable attention and opportunities for conversation with parents and other adults during infancy is likely to result in the greatest possible development of abilities in the child and adult.

3

The pre-conceptual sub-stage

Period IIA, the period of preparation for concrete operations, covers the transition from sensori-motor structures
of intelligence to operational thinking. Throughout the
sensori-motor period infants are concerned only with their
immediate environment, they co-ordinate movements and
perceptions to achieve short-term goals, but they cannot
quickly survey possible actions, assess the efficacy of alternative techniques or act to achieve a goal which is distant
in time or space. During the first part of period IIA, in the
pre-conceptual stage, the ability to represent one thing by
another increases speed and range in thinking, particularly
as language develops; but because language is acquired
slowly and does not immediately take the place of action
thinking remains to a considerable degree tied to the children's actions. This stage extends from about eighteen
months or two years to about four-and-a-half years and
corresponds approximately with the age range in English
Nursery Schools.

Although ability to represent one thing by another enables a child to use language, to interpret and draw
pictures, to extend his range in play in symbolic or constructional games and, later, to read and to write, he is
still unable to form true concepts. That is to say, he does
not assign a word to one class of objects but to a number

39

of rather similar actions or experiences and he does not do even this consistently:

Obs. 101a. J. uses the verbal sign 'tch tch' for anything that appears and disappears when she is looking out of a window in a moving vehicle as well as to her father playing peep-bo with her.

Obs. 102. At 1;0(0) T. says 'tata' to all successful actions; e.g. getting hold of a toy with a string on it, or finding an adequate response to an attempt at imitation. 'Daddy' is anyone who lights a pipe or who stretches out his arms as his father does, while 'Mummy' is used as a term expressing desire for something. (Piaget, 1951.)

In each of these cases the child has developed a verbal schema which is mid-way between a sensori-motor schema and a conceptual schema; they are sensori-motor schemas in process of becoming concepts. It is true that there is already partial dissociation from the child's activity, but the verbal sign used is an individual one which varies in meaning, in place of the fixed socially accepted verbal sign.

Variability in meaning is shown more clearly by a series of observations of Lucienne.

Obs. 101(b). L. at 1;3(4) said 'ha' to a real cat and then to a toy elephant, but not to a hen or a horse. But at 1;3(19) 'ha' had become 'haha' and referred to all animals except the cat and the rabbit, to all kinds of people and even to her sister. The rabbit was 'hin' and became identified with the cat, for which the same term was therefore used. (Piaget, 1951.)

Corresponding with the variable use of words there is also some variability in meaning. In particular, it seems that with people, the same individual may be seen as a number of distinct persons according to the clothes he wears, the place he occupies, or whether he is viewed in a mirror or photograph, and he is thought of as a succession of individuals instead of having one identity throughout his life:

Obs. 106(a). On coming in from a walk, J. said she was going to see 'Daddy, Odette and Jacqueline in the glass' as if 'Jacqueline in the glass' was someone other than herself (although she could recognize herself very well in a mirror). Again at 2;7(12), seeing L. in a new bathing suit, with a cap, J. asked: 'What's the baby's name?' Her mother explained that it was a bathing costume but J. pointed to L. herself and said 'But what's the name of that?' (indicating L's face) and repeated the question several times. But as soon as L. had her dress on again J. exclaimed very seriously 'It's Lucienne again' as if her sister had changed her identity in changing her clothes.

Obs. 106(b). . . . L. at 2:4(28) was looking at a photograph of J. when she was younger. 'Who is it?'—'It's J. when she was small'—'No, it isn't.'—'Isn't it J. when she was small?'—'Yes, when she was Lucienne.'
at 3;2(20) we passed a man: J. inquired 'Is that man a daddy?'—'What is a daddy?'—'It's a man. He has lots of Luciennes and lots of Jacquelines.'—'What are Luciennes?'—'They're little girls and Jacquelines are big girls.' (Piaget, 1951.)

Even from this brief selection of observations, it is evident that the children's verbal concepts lack the generality of true concepts. Although J. prefers to talk of 'lots of J.s and L.s' rather than of lots of girls, the people have less individuality, i.e. they are less identical with themselves than in the later stages.

Piaget suggests that the individual person, or objects, may be represented by an image and because an image has an unalterable quality (in contrast with the verbal sign which represents a 'typical individual' in a more general sense) it may well be that the differences from it are more important to a young child than are similarities in the same individual on different occasions.

As representative thinking develops, so language is used to recall events and then to describe objects or actions.

Jacqueline was first observed recalling events at the age of nineteen months:

> Obs. 104. At 1:7(13) she was in bed in the evening when it was quite dark and was sitting up talking to herself, unaware that I was listening. 'Look, look, Uncle G., Aunt A., Uncle G.' Then she stopped and lay down saying to herself, 'Nono'. After that she sat up and began again: 'Look, Mummy, Daddy, Grandma, Uncle G., etc.' going on for fully ten minutes. Two months later she felt the need to introduce things and people by name to anyone who came into the room and, talking to herself, named objects or described their actions.

> Obs. 105. At 1:9(24), for example, I heard her say to herself: 'What's that, Jacqueline, what's that?' . . . then, (knocking down a block) 'What's falling? A block' (then touching a necklace) 'Not cold' etc. (Piaget, 1951.)

The importance of language in the development of thinking is also shown in an experiment by Luria and Yudovich (1966). Identical twins, aged 5 years, who were severely retarded in speech both learned to talk while playing with different groups of Nursery School children but the slightly less able one received special training in speech. After ten months the trained boy excelled his twin in description of pictures, in constructional play, in capacity to play a role or to make objects do so, and in ability to classify objects. As the training received is not described it is difficult to assess the experiment; but it suggests that language may play a larger part than had been supposed in the development of abilities normally described as 'non-verbal'.

Imitation, play and rules

Whereas pre-conceptual thinking results from an equilibrium between assimilation and accommodation, play and imitation show a predominance of one or the other. A diagram (from Piaget, 1951) shows how Piaget conceives the development of play, imitation and thought. Successive adaptations to the environment appear in sensorimotor intelligence, pre-concepts, intuitive thinking and finally in operational thinking. But, when a child in the pre-conceptual stage cannot immediately understand a new experience he either assimilates it in phantasy without

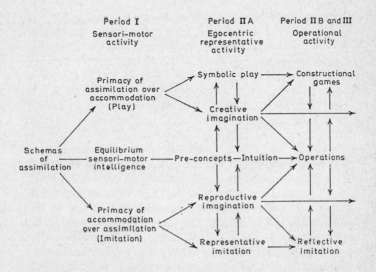

accommodating it, or accommodates his activity or his representation to models, by imitation, drawing, etc., without immediately assimilating them. As the child advances to later stages in thinking the attempt to adapt to the environment increases while symbolic play and representative imitation decrease in frequency.

Piaget sees the role of play as far more than preparation for adult activities. The pre-exercise theory which suggests that play is just this, fails to account for such observations as L. (Obs. 80. Piaget, 1951), who pretended to be a church, imitating the rigidity of the steeple and the sound of bells, or J. (Obs. 86), who lay motionless like the dead duck she had seen on a table. Piaget considers that such games either reproduce what has struck the child, evoke what has pleased him or enable him to be more fully part of his environment. 'In a word,' he says, 'they form a vast network of devices which allow the ego to assimilate the whole of reality i.e. to integrate it in order to relive it, to dominate it or to compensate for it.'

Both symbolic and imitative schemas show a development in the kind of assimilation which takes place. At first the young child projects symbolic schemas onto new objects, for example, J. (Piaget, 1951) at 1;6(30) says 'cry cry' to her dog and imitates the noise of tears. In the following days she does so with a toy bear, a duck and even a hat.

Similarly, in imitating, at 1;7(12) she pretends to 'phone, then makes her doll 'phone and in successive days rolls a leaf into a 'cornet' to use as a 'phone. Somewhat later the children assimilate one object to another; for example, at 1;9(3) J. seizes an empty bottle and makes it move, saying 'automobile'. In imitating, she assimilates herself to others; thus at 2;4(8) she is her mother saying, 'It is Mummy. Kiss Mummy' and embraces her father. At 2;8(5) she arrives in the room on all fours, saying, 'miaou'. A further development occurs as the child attempts to accommodate more and more distant objects, or to assimilate real events by means of symbolic fiction. At 2;1(9) J. puts her doll's head between the rails of the balcony and recites to it what it 'can see': 'You can see trees, etc. . . .' And, at about the same age, she tells a story to herself about a disobedient boy to persuade herself to obey an injunction not to go into the kitchen.

In this stage imitation is largely unconscious. A child reproduces and simulates movements and ideas of other persons without realizing that he does so. He takes his ideas for a drawing from his neighbour but indignantly denies that he copied; and, when something is explained or shown to him which he is to do immediately afterwards, he imagines that he has discovered for himself what in reality he is repeating from a model. Seen from a social point of view, this is egocentric behaviour in which the child confuses the I with the not-I and his own activity with that of other people.

It might be supposed that he would immediately learn to follow rules of games by imitation, but Piaget's observations show that children do not usually obey rules until they are nearly seven years old. They become aware of rules from older children, and may recite or explain some rules; for instance, that to play marbles one must make a square; but they do not know how to determine who should begin, take no account of the number of marbles they have initially, and think that 'winning' consists in hitting a marble. So Baum (at $6\frac{1}{2}$) (Piaget, 1932), says to Piaget's query 'Who has won?', 'I have and then you' since they each hit some. A young child desires only to throw a marble at other marbles; his pleasure consists in practising his skill, and, since this can be practised in company while each child plays his own game, no question of winning or rules arises.

There is some evidence that rules develop spontaneously. Infants or young children take pleasure in regularity of an action. J. at 3;4 (Piaget, 1932) experiments with marbles, dropping and throwing them and using them in imaginative games as eggs, but constantly she returns to putting them into a hollow so that after a few days this is merely a rite. However, there is no sense of obligation as there would be with a rule and, in Piaget's view, obligation begins only when there is a relation between at least two individuals—either when a ritual, such as regular mealtimes, is imposed by adults, or when a ritual results from the collaboration of two children who strive to do something in the same way as each other. Similarly, a feeling of obligation, bringing with it a sense of guilt, appears to arise in J. at 2;10(7) (ibid.) because she cannot carry out the ritual imposed by adults of eating the usual plateful of vegetables. Her mother's allowance for her because she is unwell does not lessen the sense of obligation, because the rule is regarded as unalterable. After three years, however, she can excuse her own acts saying, 'I didn't think'; but her judgments of other children's actions remain more severe, for to make allowances for them would require a capacity to imagine their intentions and this she is unable to do.

Reasoning in the young child

The reasoning of young children does not move from universal to particular by deduction, or from particular to universal as in induction but from particular to particular, without generalization and without logical rigour. Piaget calls such reasoning *transduction*. Observations show that there is development in thinking within the stage, but that transduction is typical of reasoning in children until operational thinking is achieved. In general, this holds whether the children are discussing events at home, attempting to explain occurrences in their environment, or trying to pursue a remark they have already made. An example, from the reasoning of a backward nine-year-old illustrates the reasoning of this stage:

> P. considers that the sun and the moon are alive because they move, but not a bicycle 'because it has to be pushed', nor fire 'because it has to be made' nor rivers 'because the air makes them move along'. It would seem that P. presents a typical case of a child who identifies life with self-movement. But he denies life to the North wind although it moves by itself, 'because it doesn't talk'—'But fish don't talk and they are alive?'—'They swim' (Piaget, 1928.)

Evidently, P. has two criteria of life—self-movement and speech; but he has not considered whether both are necessary simultaneously, in which case fish would be denied life, or whether one or the other will suffice, but then the North wind would be alive. It is typical of children in this stage not to ask such questions and to remain unconscious of the inconsistencies of their thinking.

Piaget names several special cases of transduction in reasoning. Juxtaposition occurs when successive unrelated judgments are given : a large boat floats because it is heavy, a small one because it is light, a raft because it is flat, a needle because it is thin, and so on. Juxtaposition may also occur in drawings. Some of the youngest children whom Piaget asked to draw bicycles drew the separate parts dispersed about the page; they appreciated that each part was necessary but were unable to represent them in relation to each other.

Syncretism, by contrast, consists in linking together things which are unrelated. It is a spontaneous tendency on the part of children to take things in by means of a comprehensive act of perception instead of considering details; they 'see', immediately, analogies between words and objects which have nothing to do with each other, and find a reason for every chance event. In short, it is a tendency to connect everything with everything else. For example J. at 2;10(8) (Obs. 111(b). Piaget, 1951), told that she cannot have oranges because they are not yet yellow says a few moments later while drinking Camomile tea 'Camomile isn't green, it's yellow already ... Give me some oranges'.

In this stage children unconsciously extend their own immediate point of view to all possible points of view. This characteristic of their thinking Piaget terms realism. It is seen when they suppose that other people see the same view of a model as they do, regardless of position, in their judgments of actions or understanding of statements beyond their experience, and in their attempts to explain physical causality or the origins of things in the world about them. It is as a result of realism that children explain events in the world by artificialism. Children constantly assert that events in the world are caused by people : J. at 2;11(7) (Obs. 115. Piaget, 1951) on seeing

47

it become light says, 'Now they've put on the light outside'. And Cli. (3.9) (Piaget, 1930) in a partly artificialized and partly magical explanation says of some clouds 'It's the mechanic who makes them go'. To him the 'mechanic' is the driver of an engine or steam engine which emits smoke; the mechanic causes the appearance of smoke and Cli. supposes that he therefore has power to control the clouds at a distance.

On the other hand the children attribute characteristics of life to objects. J. at 2;7(20) (Obs. 119. Piaget, 1951) when she was looking for her spade enquired seriously 'shall we call it' and L. at 3;7(14) (Obs. 120), when they had missed a train asked 'Doesn't the train know we aren't on it?'. At this stage children suppose that all objects are alive and can feel, that stones (and even mountains) grow, that objects know their names, and so on.

Connected with such animistic reactions are a child's ideas of causality and force which are based on his own physical or physic activity. For example, Piaget observes:

> Obs. 121. At 4;5(1), . . . L. was with me in a small boat, and we had not moved for several minutes: 'Row, Daddy, row fast, the boat's going to fall.'—'Why?'—'Because when you don't row it falls to the bottom.'—'And what about that boat in front of us (motionless)?'—'Because it's a boat on the lake, boats have to float'—'What about ours then?'—'It doesn't fall because of the oars'. . . . Then L. pressed her feet against the bottom of the boat. 'I'm putting my foot so that it doesn't fall.' (Piaget, 1951.)

These observations of Piaget's own children made at 3 or 4 years, with regard to physical causality, are very similar to those of children between 4 and 7 years which are reported in his book (1930). These children believed that things knew their names, that everything in motion could feel and that dreams came to pay them out. It may well be that as Susan Isaacs suggested (Isaacs, 1932) children argue better when they are making spontaneous observations instead of being obliged to answer questions which may interest them very little; Piaget himself observed that such concepts were much influenced by experience. The explanations given by parents and teachers may either encourage adaptation to reality or make for the continuation of mythical and magical explanations of physical phenomena; younger children in a family learn from the older ones and so are relatively better informed as to origins and causes. For these reasons, Piaget finds that stages are less clear-cut in the case of concepts of physical causality and understanding of the natural world than in the case of concepts of number, time, classes, etc., where relationship must be understood.

During this stage all but the simplest spatial relations are found difficult. In testing spatial conceptions (Piaget and Inhelder, 1951) Piaget included a sample of young children under four years; these children showed no conception of order when asked to copy a string of beads or a line of 'washing', and could not make knots. The importance of action in developing spatial concepts is suggested by a series of experiments in which the children were asked to recognize objects and shapes by handling them while unable to see them (haptic perception), to name the object, to indicate it among a collection and to draw it. Parents and teachers anticipated that the children would find it difficult to draw and might even point out the imperfections of their own drawings, but the experiments showed that, in addition, they did not know what to feel for; evidently, they lacked a mental representation of the objects and relationships of their parts. The youngest children merely held objects or moved them between their palms. In this way, they could recognize the most familiar objects such as a ball but they were unable to recognize plane shapes. Those children who did recognize some shapes did so by noticing their topological characteristics: the presence or absence of a continuous boundary and

49

holes within the shape, for example, but were unaware of Euclidean properties such as number of sides, vertices or parallels:

> Ani. (3.5) recognizes pencil, key and comb immediately. She is then given a circle which she takes in both hands and touches in a random fashion (rubbing it between her palms, etc.). Ani. seems to recognize it, but later points to a circle when she is touching a square. 'You are quite sure that this one (square) is the same as that (circle)?' —(First she holds it between her palms, fingers splayed out, then begins to turn it about.)—'Yes, quite sure.' She is then shown the circle and the square and is asked to draw them. She draws two closed figures, both elliptical and similar to each other except that the square is elongated slightly. (She has both models in front of her.)

At about 3½ years when asked to copy a short line of beads the children matched individual items but failed to put them in the correct order, at best getting adjacent pairs correct regardless of the overall sequence.

In contrast to these difficulties in unfamiliar tasks, the reasoning of Piaget's own children was often correct in situations where understanding could be achieved by practical schemas which have become generalized as a result of previous experiences:

> Obs. 112(a). At 2;4(16): When I was called and did not reply J. concluded: 'Daddy didn't hear'. At 2;4(27) in the bathroom: 'Daddy's got hot water, so he's going to shave'. At 2;6(26) we went to look for 'the slug'. 'Shall we see it today?'—'Yes'—'Why?'—'Because it isn't sunny'. The next day: 'Shall we see them?'—'No, because it's sunny'.

or

> Obs. 112(b). L. at 3;1(3): 'You're going to see Mummy so you're not coming to see me' and at 3;10(24) looking at three chairs: 'I think that one (the medium size) is big enough for J. so Cl. can sit on that one' (the big one). (Piaget, 1951.)

In the last observation L. has matched two series although this is not usually achieved until some three or four years later, but with only three girls and three chairs she can match practically; if the relationships need to be made mentally it is an impossible task at this stage. Similarly only relationships in space and time which can be appreciated practically are made correctly; all that is beyond immediate, individual space and time still has to be assimilated into representative schemas.

Implications for Nursery School teachers

Nursery School teachers who read this account of Piaget's observations may well recognize in his descriptions the behaviour of some of the children they teach. Some of them may well decide that their admirably equipped schools provide for every kind of activity which Piaget mentions and that these, together with the stories and rhymes and free activity which occupy much of the rest of the school day, allow both for the development of vocabulary and of all the kinds of symbolic representation which are characteristic of mental development in this age-group. Many Nursery Schools are well equipped and do excellent work. There is provision for a wide variety of activities: extensive play areas with large toys in which children learn to control their actions and to obtain a working knowledge of spatial relationships; a diversity of smaller toys and apparatus for construction or for use in imaginative play and for sorting, grading and counting by the older and more advanced children; domestic toys in the Wendy House and clothes for 'acting' which encourage imitation and playing of roles; and water, sand, bricks, drawing materials and paints which give opportunity for a diversity of construction and representation This is a more stimulating environment than most homes can provide and offers, in addition, the benefits of companionship.

Although activity forms the basis for thinking, it is the directive function of speech enabling mental activity to replace action which characterizes human development. In this achievement parents and teachers play important roles; for, as we have already observed, it is, on the average, children who receive most adult attention—only children and eldest children—who acquire the largest vocabularies and who become capable of the highest attainment. Studies in Russia by Luria (1959 and 1961) show how gradually control by commands and instructions supersedes the immediacy of action. Thus between 1;2 and 1;4 children will hand the experimenter the object he asks for provided that there is no conflicting stimulus; but, supposing that a child is asked to find a toy fish at some distance from him in the same line with a gaily coloured toy cat which is nearer, the request for the fish results in him stretching his hand towards it, seeing the cat and grasping that instead. Thus, Luria says:

> The directive function of the word will be maintained only up to the moment when it comes in conflict with the conditions of the external situation. While the word easily directs behaviour in a situation which lacks conflict, it loses its directive role if the immediate orientational reaction is evoked by a more closely located or brighter, or more interesting object . . . It is only at the age of 1;4 to 1;6 that this phenomenon disappears and the selective effect of words is maintained . . .

By the end of the second year visual signals gain precedence over motor connections. If an infant has several times retrieved a coin from beneath a cup on his left and then sees it hidden under a tumbler on his right he no longer repeats the motor habit he has formed but follows the visual signal and successfully retrieves the coin from beneath the tumbler. However, it is a different matter when visual signals are replaced by verbal ones. When told 'The coin is under the cup . . . Find the coin!' the younger children proved incapable of executing the instruction in an organized way; for if the verbal instruction was changed without altering the intonation, to 'Now the coin is under the tumbler . . . Find it!' the great majority of children up to two years repeated their previous action.

The kind of speech that involves more complicated preliminary connections—those which precede the action and organize it in advance—proved still more difficult to follow. Luria reports that its development occupied the entire third year and part of the fourth year of life. In a series of experiments in which children were instructed to press a rubber ball when a red light flashed but not to do so when the light was blue, children of 2;8 to 2;10 had no difficulty in pressing when the light flashed but were unable to stop the movement, very soon beginning to press the ball regardless of the signal. Even the repetition of instructions proved powerless to stop the motor excitation which had begun. However, if each flash of the red light is accompanied by the word 'Press' while each blue flash is accompanied by the command 'Don't press' the immediate verbal command is readily obeyed. But, if it was the child himself who was invited to speak the commands, children under three expended so much energy in uttering the words that the associated motor reaction became extinct. Evidently the children of this age could not create a system of neural processes that included both verbal and motor links and thus their words did not play a directive role. Between three and three and a half children accompanied their own positive command by the correct action but in uttering the negative command 'Don't press!' pressed the ball even harder. Thus the command had an immediate impulsive impact unrelated to meaning. Luria concludes that the directive influence of a child's own speech at this stage still has a non-selective non-specific character. It was not until four to four and a half years that the verbal response 'Don't press!' acquired the inhibitory effect specific to speech. At this point external speech became superfluous, for the directive role was taken over by inner connections.

Although it seems probable that these developments appear, and in the same order, among English-speaking and European children it would be rash to assume it. There is so much evidence of the influence of cultural differences on mental development that results in Russia need not necessarily be exactly paralleled among children of the same ages elsewhere. For example, findings by Piaget as to egocentricity among French-speaking children in explaining scientific phenomena did not correspond with those among English-speaking children in America and England. Russell and Dennis (1939), Oakes (1947) and Deutsche (1937) all found that even very young children showed many fewer instances of animistic and anthropomorphic beliefs and gave many more truly scientific explanations than did the children tested by Piaget. Perhaps this is due to difference in language. Use of masculine and feminine in naming objects, or reflexive verbs which imply that objects perform some action on themselves, may encourage such beliefs. Or the difference may be due to the passage of time in which scientific ways of thinking have become more common. Mead (1932) found among the Manus that total absence of animism was combined with sound appreciation of physical causality among very young children; but the Manu children were excluded from religious ceremonies, were not told traditional tales and were expected to have sufficient understanding of physical causality to handle a boat intelligently at two or three years. However, the extent of Mead's investigation was too limited to show conclusively that this kind of egocentricity was culturally determined.

An important directive function of speech which has not so far been studied in detail is that of 'moral' commands. We would expect that this would closely follow the internalization of verbal instructions except that children will generally wish to guide a chosen activity effectively, whereas they may have no desire to follow conventionally determined behaviour. In this case the role of the adult, or older children, is of even greater consequence. The writer has observed the beginning of this kind of learning in an infant of fifteen months who was fascinated by books, but had been told not to touch those in a strange house. She stretched her hand towards one, said, 'No, Elizabeth' and withdrew the hand; but, still seeing the books, repeated the sequence several times until their attraction proved so great that she took one. At this point the book was removed from her and repetition of the command in her mother's firm voice sufficed to reinforce it for the time being. If at this point the command had not been repeated, or a lax and undecided parent had repeated the command but had nevertheless allowed the child to take the book, internalization would almost certainly have been delayed. With sufficient inconsistency on the part of authority figures a habit of ignoring commands or a state of insecurity, or both, could well be built up.

On the other hand, there is the opposite danger that habitual actions may result in a needless, or even harmful, sense of obligation. Piaget observed this in Jacqueline when she could not eat her vegetables. In a child so young it may be that permission to change an habitual action has little directive effect compared with the strength of the mental processes which control the psychomotor habit. At a later age, although much behaviour inevitably remains habitual it should become accessible to verbal directions and to discussion; yet we see in psychological disturbances that this does not appear to be the case and even in normal, intelligent adults flexibility in action and thought may be severely limited and certain patterns of behaviour may unreasonably be regarded as inviolable. Perhaps one factor in such instances is that actions have not been adequately linked with verbal instruction or explanations but have remained relatively unconscious. If so, it stresses the importance of giving children reasons why behaviour is acceptable and being willing to discuss it rather than to insist on blind obedience.

All the evidence suggests that, in addition to provision of a stimulating environment, attention from adults and older children especially in answering questions and in conversation is immensely important to development in this stage. It is in these respects that many children from poor environments suffer: there are insufficient Nursery classes and in those which exist there are too few adults to give the personal attention which these children need. If it is impossible to provide more teachers, then more frequent visits from students or regular visits by senior girls studying homecraft would be beneficial. The advantages to infants and to older girls would be mutual; and, if the girls learned to become more intelligent mothers there would be lasting and cumulative benefits. When the recommendation of the Plowden Report (1967) that the number of Nursery Schools should be increased is implemented, it will not only benefit infants during their early years but should have a lifelong effect on their capacity to benefit from education.

4

The intuitive sub-stage

We have already seen in Chapter 1 that in the intuitive stage (which extends from about $4\frac{1}{2}$ to about 7 years) there is a development which enables children to begin to give reasons for their beliefs and actions and to form some concepts, but their thinking is still not operational. That is to say, they still cannot make comparisons mentally but must build them up one at a time in action. In the absence of mental representation their thinking is dominated by immediate perceptions, consequently their judgments suffer from the variability typical of perception. It is characteristic of perception that it is centred, i.e. only one feature or small area can be touched or viewed at a time; in the case of visual perception, for example, it has been shown that the centre of the field of vision is overestimated in comparison with the surrounding features and that large areas, since they catch the eye most frequently, tend to be overrated in importance. Similar distortions may occur in judgments based on tactile, kinaesthetic or auditory perceptions. It follows that perceptions of an object are variable even in the same person from moment to moment and take a different form according to the surroundings in which the object is viewed. Thus, although it is possible with practice to co-ordinate a number of perceptions of the same object by a form of perceptual activity, it is not possible to achieve the stability and reversibility of conceptual thinking which derives from mental operations.

Inability to keep in mind more than one relation at a time results in numerous limitations in thinking. Firstly, children make no effort to stick to one opinion or any given subject. It is not that they believe what is self-contradictory, but they adopt opinions successively, which if they were compared would contradict each other; and they forget the points of view which they previously adopted. On one occasion a child will say that a large lake was hollowed out and filled with water from taps, on another that it was filled by rain—and then he may revert to the first explanation again. Piaget found (1926) that the disappearance of this kind of confusion coincided with the appearance of genuine argument. Collaboration in work and play gives rise to discussion which becomes internalized as reflection, or comparison of different views in internal debate; but this does not occur until thinking becomes operational.

Secondly, there is a lack of direction in children's thinking. As we have seen in the previous stage, they juxtapose successive unrelated explanations of the cause of an event. If we ask a child how an aeroplane can fly, he lists the parts: 'the engine, the wings, the tail, etc.' To him they are all equally causes, which are interchangeable. On the other hand, he may use analogy; for example Roy (aged 8) (Piaget, 1928) explains that the moon grows. 'Half the moon (the crescent) becomes the "whole" ', and when asked how it grows, replies 'Because it gets bigger'—'How does it happen?'—'Because we grow ourselves'—'What makes it grow?'—'The clouds'—'How did it begin?'—'Because we began to be alive,' etc. But he is not arguing 'logically', 'the moon, wind, etc. are analogous to us. We grow and walk. Therefore they do,' but rather feels a direct 'relation' —which to him is sufficient reason. This is an example of syncretism. Both juxtaposition and syncretism continue

58

because a child cannot yet imagine an ordered sequence of events.

Consequently an order of events may actually be reversed in children's explanations. This is less likely in explanations which they offer spontaneously, but when children are asked to complete sentences there are frequent inversions; e.g. Don (aged 6) 'I've lost my pen because [I'm not writing]' or a backward child says Mor. (9;1): 'I am not well because [I'm not going to school].' It seems that the first relation which comes into their heads refers to consequences not to causes; and they do not in any cases realize when they are being required to explain and when to justify. Indeed, they do not consider what kind of connection is implied but feel only that some kind of relation is expressed by 'because'.

Thirdly, their thinking remains egocentric. Not only do they argue from particular to particular, by transduction, but they attribute life and feeling to objects, and believe that natural phenomena are made or controlled by men. Their thinking remains for the most part inaccessible to discussion, but subject to unconscious imitation or to suggestion. Thus Roy (8;7) (Piaget, 1928) states that we think 'with our brains'—'Who told you?'—'No one . . .' 'Where did you learn that word?'—'I've always known it' —etc. And a child who at first says he does not know what the moon is made of is shown a watch, and says that it is made of gold,—'And the moon?'—'Also gold'—'Since when did you know that?'—'I've always known it'—'Did someone tell you or did you find out alone?'—'I found out alone'—'Since when?'—'I've always known'—etc. Evidently they are not in the habit of observing the progress of their own thinking.

Fourthly, inability to see simple relations makes it impossible to compensate two relations, or to make even the simplest relations between relations. The relation of being a brother to a sister proves confusing because it is reciprocal. For example, Jacq. (7;6) (Piaget, 1928) is asked,

'Have you any brothers?'—'Two' (Paul and Albert)—'Has Paul any brothers?'—'No'—'You have two brothers?—Then Paul has some brothers?'—'No'—etc. 'And has your sister any brothers?'—'Two' (he leaves himself out)—and, an hour later after an explanation which he appeared to understand, 'Has Albert any brothers?'—'One (Paul).'

Relations between classes, or between a whole and its parts, present similar difficulties. At five years, usage of the words 'some' and 'all' is confused, about a year later 'some' acquires the absolute sense of 'few'. Fab. (6;10) (Piaget, 1959) says, ' "Some" are several. One or two are not "some", some is 3 to 100' while Cas. (6;1) asserts that '1, 2, 3, are some or several'—'And 5?'—'That's a lot.' But in taking collections of objects, usage of 'some' may not be in line with the child's own definition. Similarly, even in familiar situations a part seems to be regarded as a separate entity: Ober. (8;2) (Piaget, 1928) says 'I live in Freiberg which is in Switzerland, but I am not Swiss. It's the same thing for the Genevans.'—'Are there Swiss people?'—'Yes' —'Where do they live?'—'I don't know' and Mart. (9;5) asserts 'Geneva is in Switzerland, and Switzerland is bigger than Geneva, but you cannot be in both at the same time.'

Other terms, similarly, are shorn of their relativity: bigger and smaller, right and left, north and south, friend and enemy, are all given absolute meanings. Each distortion arises from inability to make relations mentally. A child uses 'big' and 'small' without confusion, since they imply one single comparison, whereas 'bigger' and 'smaller' have meaning only in a sequence; right and left must be understood, not only in relation to himself, but in relation to other persons or objects; and an 'enemy' or 'friend' must be seen not just as 'a horrid person' or 'someone who is kind to you' but as possibly reversing his role with respect to somebody else.

Imitation, play and rules

During the intuitive stage games of pretence begin to decline in frequency. Instead of using one thing to represent another in phantasy children begin to imitate reality : they arrange scenes of family life with dolls, attempt to construct accurate models and, in collective play, imitate events in family life, shopping, travelling in public vehicles, etc. Even in isolated play relative order supersedes the disorder of the earlier stages.

Although the children do not yet take much part in games with rules—preferring as before merely to exercise skill—they are aware of rules and believe them to be absolute. For example (Piaget, 1932) Pha. (5;6) is asked, 'Do people always play like that?'—'Yes, always like that.'— 'Why?'—"Cos you can't play any other way.' Geo. (6;0) believes that the rules were given by the 'Gentlemen of the Commune' (the town council) and that if rules were changed these gentlemen would already know any possible changes. When asked to invent new rules he does so. But assured that 'the Gentlemen of the Commune' do not already know his rules, he depreciates his own game, feeling that only what is known to them is correct. Even Ber. at so late an age as 10 years who believes it possible to change rules, asserts : 'that would be cheating'.

At first sight these beliefs may appear at variance with the practice of the children who play as they please, making as it seems any rules they like. But, says Piaget (Piaget, 1932):

> Is this contradictory? If so only in appearance. If we call to mind the peculiar mentality of children of this age, for whom society is not so much a successful cooperation between equals as a feeling of continuous communion between the ego and the Word of the Elder or Adult, then the contradiction ceases . . . the little child cannot differentiate between the impulses of his own fancy and the rules imposed on him from above.

In short this is a further manifestation of the child's egocentricity.

Moral judgments are tied to similar absolute rules of behaviour, and are subject to comparable confusions.

Naughtiness is judged by the consequences of an action rather than by intention (ibid.). Geo. (6) judges it more naughty to break eleven cups due to an accident than to break one by clumsiness while stealing jam. Const. (7) takes into account her intentions when judging her own acts but judges like Geo. of other children's actions. Again, intention is not taken into account in exploring what it means to lie. Clai (6) considers it a lie to say $2+2=5$ although he has been told that the boy who said it made a mistake, while Mab. (6) equates lies with nonsense, even when they are invented for a joke. The same attitude results in children at this stage considering it worse to tell a lie which is incredible than to tell one which might be believed. Thus Fel. (6) and other six-year-olds, judge a little girl who said that she saw 'a dog as big as a cow' worse than one who reported falsely that she received good marks at school—'because it could never happen'. 'Because it is the biggest lie.' Their reason that lies should not be told is 'Because God punishes them.' 'You get punished.' If lies were not punished, then, they say 'We could tell them.' While a six-year-old at the Maison des Petits, asked of a lie she had told whether it was right, replied, 'It doesn't matter, my mummy can't see!' During this stage, for obvious reasons, it is considered worse to tell lies to adults than to children.

Asked to recommend or to assess punishments the children suggest or approve retribution. The mother who denies cake to the daughter who is often disobedient, while giving it to the obedient child, is considered to act fairly. Indeed, retributive justice which results in punishment for wrong-doing is believed to be immanent in the Universe—told of a boy who stole apples, who later fell into the river from a broken bridge (ibid.) children said, 'It serves him right. He shouldn't have stolen,' and asked whether he would have fallen in had he been honest, they gave such answers as: 'No, because he didn't have to be punished.'

The beginning of conceptual thinking

Concepts of the world and of physical causality. We have seen that in general the child's view of the world is still egocentric. His explanations of natural phenomena and of causality in the intuitive stage are not very dissimilar from those of the previous stage. However, on the average, at the later ages the children give more artificialist explanations and fewer animistic or magical ones, supposing that even the sun was made by men; they pay more attention to detail, listing all parts of a machine, rather than immediately attributing its motion to the most obvious source of power (fire in an engine, pedals in a bicycle, . . .); they cease to believe that their own activity has the power to make objects move (the sun and clouds for instance) but shift the centre of force to the objects—believing that they move of their own accord or, alternatively, that they choose to obey man or God.

That the centre has shifted from the children's own activities to that of the objects themselves is shown by numerous examples; but as objects are believed to act on behalf of men or in obedience to them, the child confuses moral with physical causality.

Asked why a boat floats whereas a little stone which is lighter sinks immediately, Vern. (6) reflects and then says: 'The boat is more intelligent than the stone'—'What does "to be intelligent" mean?'—'It doesn't do things it ought not to do' . . . 'And is the sun intelligent?'—'Yes, because it wants to make things warm' . . . 'Is the moon intelligent?'—'Yes, because it shines at night. It lights the streets, and hunters too, I think, in the forests.' Giam. (8;6) supposes that stars are to show what the weather will be like 'If there are stars it is going to be fine.' Van. (6) asked: 'Why is it dark at night?' answers 'Because

63

we sleep better, and so that it shall be dark in the rooms.'

The case of shadows is also of interest. Where in the previous stage shadows occurred by direct participation with other shadows (shadows indoors coming from 'the trees' or from 'the night' etc.) at this stage shadows emanate from the objects, though in no particular direction. Leo. (7) thinks that the shadow of a man 'Comes out of the person, we have a shadow inside us . . . It falls onto the ground.' Mart. (8) cannot predict which side a shadow will fall but says 'It likes best to be on this side.' Jacqueline (Piaget, 1951) at 5;7(22) seeing that it was already dark at the bottom of the valley while the mountains were still in sunshine, said 'You see, the dark comes from down below. It is the water that makes the dark, it's the stream.'

In somewhat similar fashion names are thought to emanate from objects—one has but to look at an object to know its name. Fert. (7) asked how the Saleve got its name replies 'From the mountain'—'When the first men came, how did they know the sun's name?'—'Because it's bright.'—'But where does the name come from?'—'By itself.' Stei. (5;6) says of the moon 'People know it is called the moon because they had seen it'. The name is believed to be 'inside' the object, i.e. to be an essential part of it. In a long discussion with Fert. about the name of the sun (Piaget, 1929) Piaget brings him to the point of saying 'the name is in the head' (without any conviction) —'Aren't you sure?'—'No'—'Why do you think it is in the head?'—'Because it is in the sun.' So, like primitives who conceal their true names, fearing that those who know their names will have power over their persons, these children believe that the name is a part of the essence of the thing. Bo. (6;6) sums up their feeling in conversing with a friend, 'If there weren't any words it would be very awkward. You couldn't make anything. How could things have been made?'

Such a belief may well be related to the part language plays in internalizing thought. We have already seen in

Chapter 1 that young children use language in monologue
to accompany action, and that it is at least partly by this
means that they internalize commands and instructions.
Until language is internalized in thought, 'thinking' is tied
to the activity of speaking or listening. For example J.
says:

> Obs. 125 at 6;7(4) . . . 'Yes, it's my mouth which gives
> me ideas.'—'How?'—'It's when I talk my mouth helps
> me to think.'—'But don't animals have thoughts?'—
> 'No, only parrots a little bit, because they talk a little.'
> (Piaget, 1951.)

Evidently words are not thought of as having social and
mental origins but as having external reality: to see an
object is enough to make one instantly think of the word.
It follows that names are unalterable because they are
intrinsic parts of the objects, and that names as well as
things have properties—the name 'wind' has 'strength' for
example.

Number, time and quantities. The aspect of intuitive thinking most in evidence in children's solutions of problems
with number and quantities is their inability to hold in
mind more than one relation at a time. In Chapter 1 we
saw that in the intuitive stage children lacked a mental
structure which would enable them to conceive a series
of squares, seeing each pair in relation before proceeding
to the next. In the absence of mental operations children
depend on perceptual judgments and 'centre' on one
aspect or relation in a problem. They judge one group of
objects more numerous than another simply because it
covers more space, disregarding the number although they
may previously have matched the objects in two equal
lines. But they are incapable of reversing the movement of
the objects to 'see' them in two equal lines again; and
matching to these children does not necessarily imply
equality of number. Valentine (1942), for example, noticed

that one of his sons counted eight boys riding donkeys in a picture, but was unable to say how many donkeys there were without counting them also. The difficulties which arise as a result of this incomplete mental structure consist in inability to match accurately, belief that quantities are not conserved when form changes, inability to conceive a whole series or to match two series, failure to understand relationships between a whole and its parts or between a class and its sub-classes, and many consequent difficulties in measuring or in performing operations with quantities.

It is impossible to summarize in a few pages the relevant contents of some five of Piaget's books (1946a, 1946b, 1960, 1941 and 1952): only a small selection of his experiments can be mentioned here but a fuller account will be found in Lovell's book (1961).

Fundamental to understanding of number and measurement of quantities is the idea of one-one correspondence which, once made, is understood to be maintained despite rearrangement of the units. Piaget has shown that this notion develops gradually. At about four years children can put out sufficient eggs to fill cups, or a flower to each vase, but if the eggs or flowers are removed and clustered together the children suppose that their number is reduced or, if spread out, that the number increases. At six or seven years they are unlikely to believe that the number changes in this way if there is an obvious correspondence between the sets of objects; but if both sets consist of identical counters the children are more readily deceived. Indeed, many of the children cannot make another line of counters 'just the same' as one already made. They match by length of line, disregarding density of the counters or, if they succeed in this and one set of counters is then rearranged so that the ends of the lines no longer correspond, they suppose that the numbers become unequal. At a third level of difficulty, if beads are put in pairs, one each in a tube and a dish, children suppose that a necklace made

66

from those in the tube will be longer than a necklace made from those in the dish because, they say, 'It is tall'. Since the one-one correspondence has never really existed for them, for it cannot be observed and they cannot imagine it, they fall back as usual on a perceptual judgment.

Similarly conservation of quantities is not understood. Water poured from a short, broad glass into a tall thin one is believed to change in amount; if one of two equal balls of plasticine is flattened or broken into pieces, it is believed to weigh more, or less, than the unaltered ball; if tins of equal size but different weight are to be inserted into a trough of water in turn it is believed that the heavy one will make the water rise much higher; if one of two equal squares of paper is cut and rearranged as a rectangle, the two areas are no longer thought to be equal, and so on. Piaget found that children he tested understood conservation of number and substance at about six, of weight and area at about eight, but of volume not until about ten years. Experiments in England suggest that kind of materials used, and amount of experience, counts so much in forming these concepts that ages at which they are attained vary enormously. With certain materials forty per cent of ten-year-olds fail to believe in conservation of any kind of quantity but, granted sufficient experience, one-third of the infants may give correct answers to the same questions (Beard, 1965).

Inevitably children at this stage have no real conception of measurement. Asked to make a tower just the same as one made by Piaget—but on a table some distance away and 90 centimetres lower (Piaget, 1960) and given a stick the same height as the tower, none of the children thought to use the stick as a measure. They judged the heights visually, the younger children asserting 'You can see' and resisting any suggestions that they should measure. Older ones in this group might use a hand over the top of each tower, or point the stick from one to the other, ignoring differences in bases, or judge height fairly accurately by the use of two fingers; others suggest carrying one tower to the other to make a direct comparison. But none could use the principle of measurement that if A=B and B=C then C=A, using the stick as the intermediary B.

Making series of all kinds presents difficulties to children in this stage because they can compare only two elements at a time. When they are asked to put graded sticks in order, they laboriously compare each pair of sticks until they build the whole series, but even then an obvious error may not be noticed. They may succeed in putting three weights in order because they find the heaviest, the lightest and the one in the middle, but they cannot succeed with four or more weights. Given areas to compare (Piaget, 1960) with square inches or triangles to cover them, children in this stage do not see any use for the pieces but make a judgment based on one dimension only. In repeating such experiments the writer found two seven-year-old girls who supposed that a rectangular area was larger or smaller than a square one according as its long or short edge was towards them (Beard, 1960). Characteristically of this stage, they were unaware of contradiction.

Similar difficulties are found in children's conceptions of age. Taller children are usually believed to be older and the ages of adults too may be assigned according to height or, alternatively, all adults are considered 'old'. Adults of particular importance to the children may be thought of as living indefinitely. Observations of J. show both peculiarities:

Obs. 133. At 5;11(0) when their old uncle had just got rid of a servant who was too old: 'P. left Uncle A. because she was too old and tired, didn't she? So when E. (the new young maid) is as old, she'll leave Uncle A. and he'll get someone else.'
At 6;5(9): But T. may one day be bigger than you.— 'Oh yes because he's a boy so he'll be older.' T. was seventeen days old and there was more than six years differ-

ence between J. and her little brother. (Piaget, 1951.)

In like fashion tall trees, very broad trees, or those with more fruits are judged to be 'older', but times when they were planted are thought to be irrelevant in deciding which tree is older in any given year. Duration of a journey is decided by its end-points without regard to times of departure and arrival or the actual distance traversed. At about six in some children an interesting transition stage occurs in which they see a contradiction but cannot resolve it. For example, Barbara (age 6) was asked by the writer (Beard, 1960) 'Mary was born in 1952 and her brother Tom in 1954. Who is the older and by how much?' Barbara was perplexed for she said, '54 is more than 52, so Tom is older, but 52 is before 54 so Mary was born first.' She repeated this several times; then obviously still perplexed said emphatically, 'Well 52 is before 54 but Tom is older.' She could appreciate each relation separately but could not yet co-ordinate them. But, like all problems of age, this involves co-ordinating two series—of ages and dates of birth, one of which increases while the other decreases—and is more difficult than making a single series.

The relation of a whole with its parts, or a class with sub-classes presents comparable difficulties and progress. Shown a picture of a collection of children most of whom were boys and asked by Piaget (Piaget and Szeminska, 1952) 'Are there more boys or more children?' most children could answer correctly at 6 years. But with a collection of wooden beads most of which were brown and only two white, when asked 'Are there more brown beads or more wooden beads?' children aged eight answered 'More brown beads'. [The author found that English children of seven could not answer this one at all. They merely looked puzzled.] With the less familiar material they could not imagine the brown beads simultaneously in two ways —as a separate sub-set of brown beads and as part of the

69

whole set of wooden ones—so they fell back on the easier comparison of the two sub-sets. But we shall see later that even children of 12 and 13 have comparable difficulties in other contexts.

Spatial concepts. During the intuitive stage a child's conception of space is still closely tied to his actions; but because he can see one thing in relation to another (though not yet to several others) he is able to take account of proximity, separation, order and continuity; consequently the parts of the body are drawn in correct order, for example. Relationships of surrounding and enclosure assume great importance—children attempt to show the interiors of things by 'transparency': food in the stomach, a chick in the egg, or potatoes in the ground. They draw what they know rather than what they see; it is this which Piaget terms *intellectual realism*. The same characteristic results in the drawing of a profile with two eyes, or a horseman in side-view with two legs. More complex drawings may show a jumble of irreconcilable points of view; for, although a child begins to appreciate that there are different points of view of an object, he cannot immediately see how they are related to his own position in space nor to displacements of objects in space relative to him.

When children were asked by Piaget to describe and to draw their journey to school (Piaget, 1960), most of those in this stage considered them entirely in terms of their own actions, as though these were absolute. 'Mor. (5;10), remembers only where he starts and where he finishes and that he has to go round a corner on the way. He cannot call to mind a single landmark, and the journey he draws bears no relation to his plan of the school and the surrounding district.' By contrast, 'Al. (6;1) remembers names of roads, but not their order or the places where he has to turn. His drawing is just an arc with a number of points put in haphazardly to correspond with names he can remember.' While Du. (6;4) makes a complicated drawing, referring to his turning *en route* but he does not know a single landmark and considers them so unimportant that at one time he reverses the end point of the journey without altering intervening ones. Most probably the recollections which help a child (or an adult) to picture his route are essentially practical and even motor. It is true that visual images may be employed but, as we have already seen in Chapter 2, Piaget considers that visual images themselves derive from imitations of actions.

During investigations of haptic perception in which children were asked to recognize objects and plane shapes by touch, those who had reached the intuitive stage made a fairly active exploration which enabled them to distinguish rather similar shapes, such as a circle from an ellipse; but it was not until the end of this stage that they hesitantly, and still without systematic exploration, succeeded in recognizing a rhombus or a trapezium.

From these observations Piaget concludes that the formation of mental images, or other representation of shapes, results from the abstraction of properties of shapes during a child's handling of objects. Although they learn to perceive objects or shapes as wholes in infancy (as a result of visual activity during the first five months or so), children have to learn to observe properties such as corners or parallel sides by actively searching for clues to the identity of a shape before they can recognize it among similar shapes or draw it. In brief, they build up appreciation of relationships within a shape, as in space, through memories of their active exploration of it; and this, of course, is assisted by the relevant vocabulary.

A lack of adequate mental representation is evident in copying order or knots. By four or five years children can copy the order of coloured beads on a wire, or 'washing' on a line, if their copy is an identical one; but, if they are asked to reverse the order or to copy the order from a circular wire onto a straight one, they find difficulty.

Mon. (4;9) checks each bead in turn with the model, but

in copying beads from a circular string onto a straight one he finds the correct items but places them in the wrong order. Ul. (5;8) when asked to start his arrangement of beads from the other end, in copying a line of beads ABCDEFG, says, 'I don't know how it's done. I can't do it.' He tries, finding GE, omits F, puts D (opposite D in the model) and says, 'There's something bothering me here.' At a second attempt he finds GFE but sticks again at D.

In the case of knots, children at this stage can tie one as a rule but, as they cannot perform the action in imagination, they are unable to see for instance that particular tight and loose knots are identically made. Piaget found among his sample of children (Piaget and Inhelder, 1956) that they were unable even to trace a loose knot although they were given a bead to slide along the thread. They followed the section of the string passing underneath but as soon as they arrived at the intersection crossed immediately to the upper part. However, by the end of the stage some children could trace knots of superficially different appearance.

Thus, during the intuitive stage, topological properties of space—proximities, separations, order and continuity—begin to be mastered; but the projective properties, such as shadows and sections, or the Euclidean properties of angles, parallels, similarities, and so on are rarely understood by young children and will be discussed in the next chapter.

Some implications for Infants' School teachers

Good Infants' Schools, like good Nursery Schools, provide a great variety of activities and, through free play, group work or discussions with the teacher, help to enrich vocabulary. On entry to infants' school the range of abilities among five-year-olds is already very great. At one extreme are poorly endowed children from homes in slum areas who have not attended Nursery School or a play centre; whereas, at the other, are very gifted children from homes with every advantage who have already had plenty of the experiences in action or speech which they have missed. The most fortunate group have already internalized many actions mentally, have command of a repertoire of concepts and may wish to spend much of their time in reading and writing or in doing 'sums'. Thus the teacher is soon faced with the problem of providing work at three levels corresponding with Piaget's pre-conceptual, intuitive and concrete stages. Children in the first stage need the games and activities, such as playing with sand, water and various containers which precede conceptual development and are largely unstructured, and they also require as much individual attention as possible to ensure that they develop fully the directional functions of speech; those in the second need more structured games and activities which lead to formation of simple concepts and acquisition of some skills; whereas the most advanced children already require practice in using the concepts and skills they know as well as play and structured activities leading to further conceptual development. Where children are introduced too soon to any kind of activity the probability is that they will become confused and develop a distaste for learning of this kind. In the past this has been particularly likely in mathematics where practice of sums has been used largely in lieu of activities leading to concept formation.

There is a danger that so soon as children talk fluently their parents and teachers may suppose that they have mastered concepts which correspond with their vocabulary. Moreover, parents who are unaware of the importance of providing varied activities may encourage children to read early, praising this more than other skills; but a psychologist using an 'intelligence' test, which samples a wide range of skills such as copying patterns, drawing of common shapes, following instructions in order or noticing absurdities, etc. will find that in some early readers verbal fluency masks inadequacies in concepts and skills which in the long run are equally important in learning. Similarly a child who is very successful in sums may perform by imitation and memory without understanding what he does. It is important therefore for his teacher to use tests and activities which expose lack of knowledge or concepts and lead to their understanding. Some of the new kinds of number apparatus can be used in this way; but, even with apparatus, such as number rods, it is possible that children will perform exercises mechanically without insight unless they are required to discuss what they do, to explain it in their own words, or to extend a process they have performed, so indicating that they understand its nature.

Since slight inadequacies in sight, hearing, or other senses can pass undetected a range of activities in teaching any concept is particularly valuable. In one school for brain-damaged children in Birmingham, for example, classification and seriation are approached in the usual way by provision of all kinds of objects and pictures to sort, or to put in order, but a special effort has been made to use materials which appeal to a wide range of senses; the sense of touch is used in distinguishing material of different kinds and that of taste or smell in sorting bottles of substances which range from sweet to bitter or from agreeable to unpleasant. In this way a variety of experiences are used to reinforce each concept.

The possibility of deliberately speeding, or aiding, the process of internalization has been investigated in Russia. Galparin and Talyzina (1961) used the same method both with normal children of six and with backward adolescents of fifteen and sixteen. The children initially engaged in activities with concrete materials, then progressed to making audible descriptions and instructions, concrete aids being gradually reduced until, finally, the concepts were interiorized in verbal form. With this approach concepts in elementary geometry which had previously proved impossible to the backward adolescents were formed almost faultlessly from the beginning. The physical responses needed to be fully developed initially and every step in forming the concept had to be worked through; but in learning subsequent related concepts some steps could be omitted and the students might begin at the stage of thinking out loud or even at the purely mental level. Thus the development from pre-operational intuitive thinking to operational thinking was facilitated. To teachers in English Infants' Schools, so systematic an approach may seem distasteful; any method which obliges a large number of children to proceed in the same way at the same pace must be less stimulating and flexible than the active and individual methods of learning now in use. But, as with programmed learning, it may be worthwhile to keep an open mind and to experiment on similar lines since this method could conceivably be of value to some children. The greatest value of the method, however, seems likely to be with older children who need practical experience as a basis to learning and who have failed to perform at a level normal for their age.

5

The sub-period of concrete operations

The 'sub-period of concrete operations' begins when formation of classes and series takes place mentally; that is, when physical actions begin to be 'internalized' as mental actions or 'operations'. The difference in the procedure of children who have reached this stage is evident in their response to the tasks Piaget set. Whereas a child in the intuitive stage puts sticks in order of size by comparing each pair in succession, children whose thinking is 'operational' survey the sticks, then rapidly arrange them in order, in most cases without any measurement at all; the whole operation is completed in seconds where formerly it took several minutes. In like fashion, a child at this stage can draw a 'smallest' or 'largest' square without needing to make intermediate members of the series; he can imagine a series of increasing lengths, outlines or areas and the actions or 'groupings of actions' required to make a series in each case. Similarly, when asked to sort shapes into ones which go together, he does so at once, taking into account various characteristics, e.g. classifying in two ways at once—by colour and by outline—where a child at the intuitive stage groups only successive pairs, failing to make whole classes. In the sub-period of concrete operations these children have in Piaget's term an 'anticipatory schema' in making either series or classes.

The beginning of the sub-period coincides with the age at which egocentricity decreases substantially and genuine co-operation with others replaces isolated play or play 'in the company of others' which is characteristic of the earlier periods. In Piaget's view the coincidence is not fortuitous. On the one hand, the activities of the previous period gradually lead to the ability for mental operations which in turn, enable a child to appreciate relationships, including those to his peers; on the other, parents and teachers increasingly provide opportunities for, and induce interest in, co-operation and enable him to correct misconceptions through discussion.

During the sub-period we shall see that children master even complex relationships. They classify, or make series, in two or more ways simultaneously, imagine views from vantage-points other than their own, measure with reference to two axes at once, appreciate the inter-relationships of a whole with its parts or a class with its sub-classes, and so on. Nevertheless thinking at the level of concrete operations shows some limitations. These appear in children's difficulties in dealing with verbal problems, their attitudes to rules and beliefs about the origins of objects and of names, their procedure by trial and error rather than by testing hypotheses in solving problems, inability to see general rules or to accept assumptions, and failure to go beyond the data provided or to imagine new possibilities or explanations. We shall follow through both their achievements and their failures from Piaget's own investigations.

Piaget lists eight groupings of relationships which children learn to deal with during this sub-period.

The simplest logical grouping of relations occurs in forming a *hierarchy of classes*. For example, the class of animals can be broken down into sub-classes: carnivore and non-carnivore; while both sub-classes can be again divided into sub-classes successively, until we arrive at the names of particular kinds of animal. The ability to understand pairs of sub-classes is commonly in demand in the work of primary schools: numbers are divided into odds and evens, into those over 10 and those less than 10, classes of words may be learned together because they obey certain rules in spelling and pronunciation, characteristics of different classes of birds are studied, e.g. those which glide and those which hover, to take only a very few examples.

Until about nine years, most children continue to find some difficulties in understanding relationships between classes. We have already met a child who could not conceive that a member of the class 'Genevans' could also be a member of the class 'Swiss'; to him an individual could not belong to two classes. But a little later in the stage, in an experiment which Piaget performed (Piaget and Inhelder, 1959) children agree that collections of roses, tulips and other flowers are all flowers but they assert that if all the flowers die, the roses (or tulips) will still remain; for them the sub-classes still have to some extent a separate existence.

A second elementary grouping of relationships depends on the ability to assemble relationships which express differences. We have seen children in the intuitive stage learning to build a sequence by seeing successive pairs in relation, so creating an *order of succession*. This, too, is an achievement constantly employed in primary schools, and frequently relearned with new kinds of materials. Again selecting a very few examples: in physical activities children may line up in order of height; in the classroom they answer their names in alphabetical order; in arithmetic they compare capacities, distances and heights, weights, areas and volumes as well as comparing various quantities by means of fractions, decimals and percentages; in studying the weather, temperatures, rainfall and pressures are compared, while in map-reading latitudes, contours of height and depths, and scales may be graded in order.

Many more examples could be given from every subject. Difficulties remain until at least the end of the primary school. If children are asked to write the numbers 1327, 2111, 1987, 5000 in order of magnitude, putting the smallest first, some intelligent ten-year-olds consider the irrelevant figures or, asked to compare areas when one is long, but thin, and another squarish, they may revert to an intuitive judgment although they have done practical work in measurement.

A third fundamental operation is *substitution*. For example, children constantly use such relations as $8=7+1$ $=6+2=5+3$ . . . in arithmetic, showing different ways of reaching the same end-result. Daily use of different combinations of coins to make the same sum, or experiences with weights, capacities and lengths of time, lead to appreciation of such relationships provided that they are substitutions seen in practice. Other alternative sub-divisions of classes are in constant use, though they may not be considered so explicitly: sub-divisions of the class of children into boys and girls, children over and under 8, those who take school dinner and those who do not, etc. or statistical sub-division of people in geography into male and female, adults and children, white, brown and black races, employed and unemployed, and so on. In each case when the first category is selected, the nature of the second (or others) must be complementary.

In terms of relations, the preceding operations give rise to reciprocity which is typical of *symmetrical relations*. By about six years children realize that a distance is unaltered in whichever direction it is measured (though they may be confused if the distance to be measured is between a tall tree and a short one) (Piaget, 1960); at about eight years most children understand that if there are two brothers then each is a brother to the other. Similarly, they begin to comprehend such relations as friends, enemies, partners in games, two factors of a number, symmetry in shapes (demonstrated by folding), etc.

Four further groupings are based on multiplicative operations, i.e. relations which are made in two or more ways simultaneously.

When a child arranges objects into sub-classes by considering simultaneously shape and colour he will arrive at four sub-classes which can be described in terms of both systems at once. e.g. red squares, blue squares, yellow squares, red circles, blue circles, yellow circles. This is a *multiplication of classes*. Many examples come to mind in children's work and play. Quiz questions such as : a yellow flower beginning with 'd'?, an even number between 10 and 20?, a continent with 12 letters south of the equator?, employ double classifications. And treble classifications are not uncommon; in a mixed class we expect 'the third boy in the second row' to identify himself, and if we provide objects which can be classified not only by colour and shape but also by texture we may reasonably expect that all normal children of nine will succeed.

In the same way a *multiplication of series* can be made. It is possible to identify a square in a street map by denoting squares in serial order alphabetically in one direction and by numerals in the other, in a method already familiar to many children of 7 or 8 in the game 'battleships'. At a later stage they learn to associate series of values of two variables in years in some primary schools using discovery methods.

A particular case is of some significance. If there are only two rows A1, A2, A3, A4, A5 and B1, B2, B3, B4, B5. for example, we have the case of a one-one correspondence, which as we have already seen is made quite early in matching counters. The one-one correspondence is important in building up concepts of time. A child must realize that an increasing sequence of ages in the class corresponds with a decreasing series of dates of birth; if John is a year older than Mary he was born a year earlier. But this is a concept which develops fairly slowly and is not achieved until children reach a mental age of nine or more. In an experiment made by Piaget in which liquid was poured in equal amounts from a spherical glass container into a cylindrical one, children of about seven and eight could draw the levels of liquid in blanks provided but they could not show how the two series of levels corresponded; though they might put the increasing sequence of levels in the cylinder in order, they still failed to match them with the corresponding decreasing levels in the sphere (Piaget, 1946b).

We have also seen that understanding of the one-one correspondence in general, precedes development of concepts of conservation e.g. conservation of number is not understood by children who cannot copy a line of counters accurately.

Finally, both for classes or series, we may group individuals by making one term correspond with several, instead of one to one, e.g. a family of brothers and their sons may be arranged in a *family tree*. In such a case the relationship between brothers is symmetrical but that between father and son is asymmetrical. Similarly, classification of shapes into triangular, conic section, and quadrilaterals, with their sub-classes results in a *family tree of classes*.

These are the eight logical 'groupings of operations' which Piaget finds become available to children during the period of concrete operations. Since they are logical, thinking which conforms to them obeys certain laws. Piaget defines five laws (Piaget, 1950).

The laws of groupings

I. When any elements of a grouping are combined they

produce a new element of the same kind: two distinct classes may be combined into a comprehensive class which embraces them both, e.g. men + women = adults. Or a series of such combinations may be made.

Algebraically, if we denote the classes by capital letters, with suffices where necessary: $A + A_1 = B$, $B + B_1 = C$, etc. This is the law of *closure or composition*.

II. Every change is reversible. Thus the two classes just combined may be separated again: adults − women = men. If numbers are substituted for classes we may say that each original operation of a group implies a converse operation: subtraction for addition, division for multiplication, etc. This is the law of *inversion*: if $A + A_1 = B$, then $A = B − A_1$ or $A_1 = B − A$.

III. Combination of operations is associative, i.e. a result obtained in two different ways remains the same in both cases. For example, $(2 + 3) + 4 = 9$, or in dealing with classes:

Boys + (girls + women) = (Boys + girls) + women.

The law of *associativity* can be expressed algebraically as $(A + B) + C = A + (B + C)$.

IV. An operation combined with its converse is annulled e.g. 3 miles north + 3 miles south = 0 miles away.

This is the law of *identity* which can be written algebraically as $A − A = 0$.

V. A class added to itself remains the same class e.g. men + men = men. This is the law of *tautology* for classes: $A + A = A$. But for numbers, since a unit added to itself produces a new number, e.g. $2 + 2 = 4$, the law is that of *iteration*: $A + A = 2A$.

It is probable that only mathematicians who read this book will wish to see how it is that the eight 'groupings of operations' obey the five laws given here. We will quote just one instance, that of hierarchy of classes, leaving them to work out the others:

'Let us suppose that a species A forms part of a genus B, of a family C, etc. The genus B includes other species besides A; we will call them A' thus A'=B−A). The family C includes other genera besides B: we will call them B' (thus B'=C−B) etc. We then have combinativity: A+A'=B; B+B'=C; etc; reversibility: B−A'=A etc.; associativity: (A+A')+B=A+(A'+B')=C, etc. and all other characteristics of groupings.' (Piaget, 1950.)

Play in the period of concrete operations

During this period there is a further diminution in the number of symbolic games and 'imaginary' companions disappear, but there is a development into theatrical entertainment. From about seven years children wish to make accurate replicas or to build models 'which work'. There is besides a development of games in which some, at least, of the eight categories of groupings are practised: classifications are enjoyed in nature study and in labelling collections of various kinds, numbers are classified in all kinds of ways for fun, car numbers are sought in serial order, greatest or least speeds, weights, etc., are recorded, symmetrical patterns are made in every variety of ways with ink-blots, paper and scissors, family trees are studied, and we have already mentioned quizzes which involve multiple classifications and the game 'battleships' which employs multiplication of series. If children in these age groups do not enjoy mathematics it is surely because teachers do not use their natural interests!

Some late misconceptions among English children

It seems that Piaget may be unduly optimistic in saying that children achieve concrete operations in most fields by 'about eleven'. Since his samples were small they may

83

not have been representative of the majority of children. In investigations made by students, organized by their mathematics lecturers through the Mathematics Section of the A.T.C.D.E., some experiments showed that 40 per cent or more of older juniors in an assortment of English primary schools still failed in some items testing understanding of conservation of quantities. We will mention only two instances here, and one experiment made by the author.

Firstly, it would be assumed that most ten-year-olds who have known such facts as 2 pints make 1 quart, for several years, would understand that a quantity of liquid merely poured from one container into several smaller ones would not increase in quantity, but be substantially the same. The students found that about 40 per cent of third-year juniors did not think so (Beard, 1963). Following Piaget's and Inhelder's experiment, some 240 children in 40 schools were shown two large glasses containing equal amounts of 'water to drink'. One amount was then poured into two smaller glasses and the children were asked whether there was still the same amount to drink in the big glass and the two smaller ones, or more, or less. Many children, especially younger ones, supposed that two glasses must hold more water. If, however, they said the two quantities were still equal, the water was poured from the two small glasses into five still smaller glasses and the question was repeated. Some children then decided that so many more glasses must hold more water. . . .

Age	4·10-5·9	5·10-6·9	6·10-7·9	7·10-8·9	8·10-10+
% correct	10·2	20·9	40·5	58·5	63·0

In a second item testing conservation of volume two identical tins were shown to the children but weighted so that one was heavier than the other. The children saw one inserted in a trough of water and watched the water rise. They were then asked what would happen if the

84

heavier tin was inserted instead. In this case less than 10 per cent of the oldest group realized that the water would rise to the same level, some children predicting that it would overflow. The author has also found similar proportions of children with misconceptions in dealing with certain more difficult concepts of weight and area (Beard, 1965).

Limitations in thinking during the period of concrete operations

Whereas misconceptions due to lack of experience may be easily corrected, limitations in verbal reasoning appear to be characteristic of the period. Here are some of Piaget's findings reported in *Judgment and Reasoning in the Child* and *Language and Thought of the Child.*

Firstly, in one of Binet's tests: 'Edith is fairer than Susan; Edith is darker than Lily; who is the darkest of the three?' Piaget found that the problem was rarely solved before the age of twelve, for until then children argued in such a way as 'Edith and Susan are fair, Edith and Lily are dark, therefore Lily is darkest, Susan is the fairest and Edith in between.' In other words, so soon as they were required to use verbal propositions instead of objects, the children considered one statement at a time, just as children in the intuitive stage considered one relationship at a time in dealing with objects.

When asked to explain absurdities children in this period proved incapable of accepting the premises and reasoning from them, or they saw only a special case without appreciating the need to express a general law. Commenting on one of Binet's absurdities: 'If ever I kill myself from despair I won't choose a Friday, because Friday is a bad day and would bring me ill luck;' children said:

'People can kill themselves any day, they don't need to kill themselves on a Friday' (Bai. 9;6).

'Friday is not unlucky' (Yan. 9;10).

85

'He doesn't know if it will bring him ill-luck' (Berg. 11;2).
'Perhaps Friday will bring him good luck' (Arn. 10;7).

In each of these cases the child refuses to admit the premises, failing to see that he has missed the point. What is required, of course, is that he should accept the premises and argue correctly to avoid the contradiction in the statement. But they fail to see the contradiction because they do not attempt to see the situation from the speaker's point of view; they cannot relinquish their own. Others attempt to justify the premises. Campa. (10;3) and Ped. (9;6) both assert 'It is a day when you must never eat meat.' A few others, again, stated 'He would do better to kill himself on a Friday, since it is an unlucky day.' So there is nothing absurd to them in the statement; but again they see it from their point of view.

In questions relating to physical causality Piaget found the same difficulty. He could not persuade children to accept a suggested assumption unless he forced them to believe it as an affirmation. Here is a typical conversation: 'If there was no air would this (an object suspended by a string which was swung round rapidly) make a draught? —'Yes'—'Why'?—'Because there is always air in the room' —'But in a room where all the air had been taken away would it make any'?—'Yes, it would'—'Why'?—'Because there would be some air left,' etc. The ability to assume the truth of a statement without believing it, just to see where it will lead to, Piaget finds does not usually appear until about 11/12 years.

Failure to see a general law also occurs repeatedly. Mor (7;11) completes the statement 'Paul says he saw a little cat eating a big dog. His friend says that's impossible, because . . .', with the assertion, 'because the little cat is little and the big dog is big.' And Baz (aged 8) completes 'half six is three, because . . .', by saying 'it has been divided'. Obviously he means it has been divided into two equal parts; but that is just what he fails to say, so he only repeats the original statement. In discussing such statements Piaget concludes (Piaget, 1928): 'Has he had in mind the propositions "Little cats do not eat big dogs" . . . or "Half 6 is 3, because 3 and 3 makes 6"? It is obvious that he has not. The child has been conscious only of the particular case to which his answer referred, and was unable to express the corresponding general laws.'

In Chapter 1 we referred to the difficulty children in this period have in explaining proverbs. They fail to see a hidden meaning but assimilate some familiar item to an experience which they already understand, or, in this case, to superficial similarity. Peril. (10;6) identifies 'Drunken once will get drunk again' with 'Whoever goes to sleep late, will wake up late,' because he says 'There are the same words in the sentence before the comma, and the words that are repeated in the two sentences are put in the same place; in both sentences there is a word that is repeated.'

To provide a meaningful definition also presents difficulty to most children before adolescence. At the intuitive stage, children define simply by the use to which an article is put—'a fork is to eat with' for example; but during the period of concrete operations children begin to define by genus, e.g. 'a mother is a lady' though without generalizing the notion; later they may give their first logical definition formulating it both by genus and specific difference (making a double classification) e.g. 'a mother is a lady who has children'. But to give such a verbal definition implies conscious realization of the use one is making of a word or a concept which in turn implies reflection and thought.

Limitations remain also in children's conceptions of origins of rules and in their moral conceptions. The increasing co-operation which sets in at 7-8 years does not immediately suffice to suppress the 'almost mystical attitude to authority' of younger children, for, as Piaget notes, thought always lags behind action in children's development. Until about ten years rules of games are still believed to be decided by adults; so to violate rules, although not impossible, is regarded as unfair. After ten years there is a change: a rule is still sacred in so far as it has been laid down by adults but children no longer feel that everything was arranged for the best in the past so that the established order must be respected; instead they believe in the value of experiment, though only if it is sanctioned by collective opinion of the peer group.

Until late into childhood, names, like rules, have an almost mystical significance. Few children realize that names were decided by people and that they could be altered: on the contrary, most children assert that names of things are given by God and that they are unalterable. Their sense of 'law immanent in the universe' does not allow them to appreciate that there are chance occurrences. They attempt to explain every coincidence.

However, the sense of comradeship among children in these age groups changes their attitude to authority, and their assessment of actions; it is as bad, or worse, to tell a lie to a comrade as to an adult; actions are now worse if motives are wrong (though the material damage is small) than when motives are good (but material damage is great). They learn to distinguish mistakes from deliberate wrongdoing and are much concerned with 'fairness' of punishments.

Spatial concepts

During the period of concrete operations, among children tested by Piaget, understanding of topological concepts was completed and projective concepts, such as perspective and sections were gradually mastered (Piaget and Inhelder, 1956). The children also began to use some Euclidean concepts; measures of length, area and angles could be applied intelligently, for example, and properties such as numbers of sides or angles, or parallel sides of a figure were observed correctly. But accurate reproduction of a model, requiring measurement from two axes of reference, ability to calculate ratios within similar figures, or co-ordination of two or more systems of reference (such as horizontal and vertical on a hillside), usually developed later. Indeed where several relations had first to be recognized and then either to be equated, as in proportionality, or seen in relation to each other, the ability did not usually develop before adolescence. Piaget and his collaborators found that the majority of pre-adolescents were unable to generalize beyond what was finite, visible and tangible; they could not conceive of a line as an infinite collection of points nor imagine successive sub-divisions of a line, or area, into indefinitely small elements.

By about seven most children begin to reverse orders easily, even in the case of an arrangement of beads in a figure of 8, and they can see similarities between knots. Gel (7;10), for instance, said of a clover knot: 'It's the same as the earlier ones but it's not pulled tight' and he describes the difference between the left- and right-handed knots: '. . . there it's on top, there underneath.'

In drawing maps they are likely to show a number of disconnected sub-sections. 'Rev. (7;10) makes a model consisting of two separate sub-groups which are quite independent—the only object which they have in common does not help him because he sees it first in one group then in the other.' But, Piaget observed 'each partial plan has been drawn with a particular vantage-point or a particular journey in mind, and each vantage-point, or journey, is still unique'. When asked to re-draw his plan as it would be, if rotated through 180°, San. (9;4) rotated the school buildings correctly and the objects near it, but he reversed another section of the plan from back to front though not from left to right, and left a third area unrotated.

Notions of perspective are absent at about seven years in most children, but are applied systematically in drawing some time after nine years. Tests by the A.T.C.D.E. Mathematics Section of children as old as ten years showed that ideas of perspective were by no means complete in

English children of that age although Piaget found them to be so in Swiss children of about nine. But among younger children, recent observations by Nursery School teachers suggest that the concept of a pilot's view, (which was understood by only seven children among sixty six- and seven-year-olds tested by the writer in 1953-5) is now quite commonly understood by children in Nursery classes. In 1964 also nearly all eight-year-olds among a sample of fifty tested by the writer understood this concept (Beard, 1968). This appears to be another example of special experiences advancing the stage of development. Teachers suggest causes such as viewing aerial photographs on television, the use of simple constructional toys which are made into models on the floor, and the study of diagrams in plan, which accompany some of these toys. But understanding of viewpoints from the opposite sides of the room, or from an upside-down position seem to be quite unaffected by these experiences and show no such rapid development over the years.

Among his experiments to test children's ability to imagine different perspectives, Piaget asked some children to predict the shapes of shadows of a stick and of a circular disc which were tilted in a succession of positions towards a screen. As usual, those in the 'intuitive' stage drew their own view. Those in a transitional stage attempted to indicate a change in shape by drawing a bent stick for the intermediate position, or one sloping across the page (as they viewed it) but foreshortened. In the case of the circle they drew circles for each position but of diminishing sizes. In a similar experiment by the writer fifty per cent of English children could draw three correct pictures of the circle at ten years, but in the case of the stick only six per cent could do so; they failed to see that the picture of the stick should be upright but foreshortened, though some drew a small circle for the horizontal position of the stick (Beard, 1968).

In measuring, the children of this period learn first to

use a large intermediary object and only later use a smaller object as a unit. When offered units of different kinds to compare areas younger children cover the areas with small squares, triangles or oblongs and count their number regardless of relative size. But by about nine years they equate two triangles to one square, and two squares to one oblong, so making an accurate comparison. In an unpublished study of children in the Birmingham area, all of a large sample of children of ten years could do this. By about nine or ten, Piaget's sample of children realized the need for more than one measurement when copying an angle or in locating a point on a page. At about ten they could locate a point in three dimensions by measuring three perpendicular lengths.

Since continuity is a difficult concept one might suppose that children would find the prediction of loci difficult also. But in experiments by Piaget, Szeminska and Inhelder (Piaget, 1960) children aged seven who had found a few points equally distant from two given ones were able to describe the locus, and were equally successful in recognizing a circular locus. Those a little older could already construct mentally the cycloidal locus of a point on the rim of a rolling wheel.

In the case of similarity some children could construct similar triangles provided that they were similarly situated, with bases parallel—but if measurement with calculation of proportion was required, even children of ten and eleven years were unable to go beyond a two-fold magnification.

Thus, parallel with ability to imagine classes and relations which depend on mental actions or operations, there is a development in mental actions which lead to a wide variety of spatial concepts; but, in both developments, children in the period of concrete operations show limitations in the number of relations they can deal with simultaneously, by their inability to generalize beyond particular cases and by failures in verbal problems.

Discussion

The possibility of operational, internalized thinking in the junior school stage should not blind teachers to the findings of Piaget and other psychologists that a large part of thinking still proceeds at the intuitive level. The danger is still very great that learning will be conducted verbally and thus fail to become attached to the activity which is essential if it is to have meaning. We have quoted instances, and could mention many more, where children up to ten years old know their tables but do not understand the related concepts: they repeat tables of weight but cannot use scales or balances, recite tables of capacity but fail to realize that volume or capacity is conserved when a quantity of sand or liquid is transferred from one container to another, or they quote equivalences between square inches and square feet although they know neither that area is conserved nor how to measure it. Piaget has shown that, for understanding to develop, the whole sequence of internalization must be complete, beginning from the activities on which all else depends. But we should also use the practical activities as tests. A child who cannot use scales or a balance, nor solve simple problems with them such as putting three weights in order, does not adequately understand the concept of weight, whether he recites his tables or not. If he does understand he will be able to give a simple explanation of what he is doing or show how to extend the activity or apply what he knows in a different situation.

It is not only the fluent way in which children use words which deludes teachers or parents into believing that they already understand concepts but also their unevenness of development. If we find that they understand concepts in some situations we tend to suppose that they will do so in similar ones, especially if these are generally considered easier. Experimental work in Britain shows that the development of any one individual is more piecemeal than

that described by Piaget; his suggestion that an overall
structure develops in any period or sub-period of development does not appear to be fully borne out. It is true that
most of the responses of one child may be recognizable as
'pre-conceptual', 'intuitive' or 'operational', but this is not
necessarily so. Even in different experiments designed to
test a single concept several levels of response may be
given by the child. Piaget himself quotes instances where
different materials made questions easier: 'children' including 'boys' and 'girls' made it much easier to understand
inclusion of one class within another than wooden beads
including brown and white ones, for example. In the
A.T.C.D.E. investigations (Beard, 1963) into concepts of
number there were children who understood conservation
of number in any one, or two, of three experiments, perhaps succeeding in the most difficult items and failing in
the easier ones; experience played a large part in what
children could do or understand. One child who counted
well failed to show understanding of any of the number
concepts but another who could not count to ten nevertheless explained one-one correspondences, conservation
of number, the relation between parts and a whole and
composition of numbers. Thus, where teachers wish to
find out what their pupils understand it is wise to use a
wide range of tests and to avoid making assumptions as to
understanding of one concept until it has been tested in
various ways.

There is evidence that retarded children tend to be even
slower in forming concepts than in other learning. A
number of studies in Birmingham University School of
Education, comparing backward children and adolescents
with primary school children have shown, as would be
expected, that the retarded children attained concepts later
than normal children did, but this proved to be true even
in terms of mental age. For example, Hood (1962) found
that whereas half of normal subjects thought operation-
ally in certain number concepts at seven years two months,

93

half the retarded adolescents failed to do so until they attained a mental age of eight years eight months. Possibly this reflects the unsuitability of arithmetic teaching to their particular difficulties. Nelson (1962) reported that allowing E.S.N. children to play with Piaget type materials improved their level of attainment in arithmetic, and Tansley (1965) with his colleagues devised exercises based on Piaget's experiments which also had a beneficial effect on the attainment of concepts of a mathematical kind. As with infants, the use of a diversity of materials appealing to senses of touch, or taste, as well as to the eye and ear can help to overcome difficulties due to slight visual and auditory defects.

A temporary cause of retardation prior to adolescence may be slow physical maturation, as is commony recognized in the term 'late-developer'. There is little evidence, however, that Piaget's stages in the development of thinking correspond with physical development. Grey Walter (1956) mentions a few changes in electrical wave impulses within the brain which correspond with one or two substages mentioned by Piaget; but Tanner (1963) failed to find physiological correspondences between Piaget's stages and physical development although he showed that maturity as indicated by an X-ray of wrist bones was related to success in the 11-plus examination. Thus, although environmental and other influences are more important, rate of maturation does influence mental development but perhaps in speed, interests and application rather than in level of thinking.

Normal children during this period of development need more carefully structured activities involving more complex relationships than do infants and, in subjects with a science bias, they profit from well-organized 'experimental' work which enables them to make their own measurements and observations and perhaps to make 'discoveries'. There is an increasing number of books which show how to introduce mathematical and scientific concepts in this way. The approach is described in some detail in publications of the Schools Council (1965), the A.T.C.D.E. Mathematics Section (1963) and the Mathematics Association (1956).

During the earlier years in the junior school children are led to form new concepts through practical activities similar to those in the infants' school but with greater complexity. When first meeting ideas of volume, a teacher may provide boxes of various sizes together with inch-cube bricks to enable children to test their impressions that one box holds more bricks than another but, at a later stage, the children may calibrate jars of different shapes, using cubic inches of water, so that they appreciate the different heights a cubic inch can occupy in different vessels, before proceeding to measure regular and irregular solids by suspending them in the jars. Through such activities they link formulae such as $V=lbh$, when they meet it or invent it, with practical knowledge of what volume is and how to measure it. The most able children may well raise questions about objects which float and pursue their inquiries through further experiments or by seeking information in science books.

For older juniors, practical work has now been devised which leads to more advanced concepts which used to be studied only in the secondary school. Thus we find nine-year-olds using Dienes' cards and apparatus 'to complete the square' of such expressions as x^2+6x. They use a square to represent x^2, six one-inch-wide strips of length x arranged in two equal rectangles on adjacent sides of the square, and so complete the square of side $x+3$ by simply filling in a square hole with unit squares. In this way, the algebra becomes concrete; an operation which is often found difficult by thirteen-year-olds using symbols is seen as simple and obvious by the nine-year-olds. However, they do not yet generalize their results; one has but to ask them what should be added to x^2+7x to complete the square to see that their understanding is limited to

95

what can easily be achieved in action. The ability to generalize experiences such as these can be facilitated by requiring the children to describe in their own words what they do, for they then have a formula to guide the action in a more difficult case. Similarly, appreciation of more complex relationships and general laws is now introduced to older juniors through graphical work derived from their experiments and their attempts to interpret or to extrapolate from their results.

An alternative way of bridging the gap to adolescent modes of thinking is to simplify the relationships which juniors are asked to appreciate. Thus, in music, the pentatonic scale of five notes, enables children to compose simple tunes, to record and to read them easily and to play them without discords. In this way, children can appreciate the art of music-making from their own experience.

The difficulties children experience in giving definitions, in solving problems or stating propositions verbally is partly met by asking them to do these things during practical work and accepting statements or definitions suitable at their level. Thus verbal expression is linked with the children's activities until it becomes possible for them to generalize to whole classes of similar experiences or to recognize in verbal problems situations similar to those which they have already learned to solve practically and to describe in terms meaningful to them.

6

The period of formal operations

Piaget believes that formal operations are initiated through co-operation with others. At the beginning of adolescence social life enters a new phase of increasing collaboration which involves exchange of view-points and discussion of their merits before joint control of the group is possible. This obviously has the effect of leading children to a greater mutual understanding and gives them the habit of constantly placing themselves at points of view which they did not previously hold. Consequently they progress to making use of assumptions. In addition, discussion gives rise to an internalized conversation in the form of deliberation or reflection. Piaget observes: 'As far as intelligence is concerned, co-operation is thus an objectively conducted discussion. . . . It is clear that co-operation is the first of a series of forms of behaviour which are important for the constitution and development of logic.' (Piaget, 1950.)

Could this development of formal operations occur without co-operation and discussion? Evidently Piaget believes that it would not:

. . . the coercions of other people would not be enough to engender a logic in the child's mind, even if the truths that they imposed were rational in content; repeating correct ideas, even if one believes that they

97

originate from oneself, is not the same as reasoning correctly. On the contrary, in order to teach others to reason logically it is indispensable that there should be established between them and oneself those simultaneous relationships of differentiation and reciprocity which characterize the co-ordination of viewpoints. (ibid.)

Consideration of many viewpoints gives adolescent thinking a new flexibility. Where a child is limited to action and a partial reality the adolescent mentally surveys many possibilities, forms theories and conceives imaginary worlds. His increasing interest in a variety of social systems, real or possible, obliges him to be critical of his own standards so that he begins to look objectively at himself and the assumptions of the various groups of which he is a member. His attitude to rules and conventions changes. Unlike the child who believes them to be unalterable, an adolescent comes to realize that they have been decided by adults and may differ among different groups of people. In games he changes rules as he wishes provided that those who play agree. His moral judgments become less extreme; for example, he appreciates that a good man may have some bad characteristics and points out what there is to be said both for and against him.

A number of other new capacities stem from the initial development in seeing many points of view. Firstly, the adolescent can accept assumptions for the sake of argument. Secondly, he makes a succession of hypotheses which he expresses in propositions and proceeds to test them. Thirdly, he begins to look for general properties which enable him to give exhaustive definitions, to state general laws and to see common meanings in proverbs or other verbal material. Fourthly, as we have already seen in his spatial concepts, he can go beyond the tangible, finite and familiar to conceive the infinitely large or infinitely small, and to invent imaginary systems. Fifthly, he becomes conscious of his own thinking, reflecting on it to provide logical justifications for judgments he makes. Sixthly, he develops an ability to deal with a wide variety of complex relations such as proportionality or correlation.

Since Piaget was able to give five rules applying to eight 'groupings' which covered the new developments in operational thinking at the concrete level, the reader may ask whether further rules can be given for formal operations. The answer is that, since the thinking is logical, it can be described in mathematical terms used in propositional logic. However, we do not intend to describe Piaget's algebraic notation here. The interested reader is referred to his books (Inhelder and Piaget, 1959; Piaget, 1926) or to a simple explanation in *The Pupil's Thinking* by E. A. Peel. Those with mathematical interests are referred also to a logician's criticisms of Piaget's choice of an algebraic notation and of his descriptions of some experiments in terms of it (Parsons, 1960).

Assumptions, hypotheses and laws

In *The Growth of Logical Thinking* (Inhelder and Piaget, 1959) the development of children's thinking to the level of formal operations is illustrated from their solutions to a number of problems. At about twelve years, children begin to reason in propositions, arguing by implication, 'If (such and such) happened you would find (some unobserved consequence)'. In classifying floating and sinking objects Jim (12;8) says, 'If you take metal, you need much more wood to make the same weight than metal.' And Wak. (14;0), in explaining how to make the shadows of rings of different sizes coincide on a screen, says, 'You may take any distance provided that the ratio is the same.' Huc. (15;6) gives a precise rule in a somewhat different form: 'For the light to make twice the size (of shadow) it takes twice the distance.' In each of these cases an assumption has been made as to a possible action and a consequence has been mentioned; thus each assumption

99

serves as a hypothesis which can be tested by an experiment.

The difference between child and adolescent in surveying possibilities is well illustrated in an experiment in which subjects were shown four large bottles and one small one each containing colourless liquids. A demonstration was made in which the liquids were combined to produce a yellow colour and another was added to remove the colour. The children were told that the liquids used had been taken from the bottles and were asked to reconstruct the experiment. Denoting liquids from the large bottles by 1, 2, 3 and 4 and that from the small bottle by g, Piaget describes one child's attempt as follows (using $\times$ for with):

Kis. (9;6) begins with $(3 \times g)+(1 \times g)+(2 \times g)+(4 \times g)$, after which he spontaneously mixes the contents of the four glasses in another glass, but there are no further results. 'O.K. we start over again.' This time he mixes $4 \times g$ first, then $1 \times g$: 'No result.' Then he adds $2 \times g$, looks, and finally puts in $3 \times g$. 'Ah!' (yellow appears, but he adds $4 \times g$) 'Oh! So that! So that's (4) what takes away the colour. (3) gives the best colour.' He is asked 'Can you make the colour with fewer bottles?'—'No.'—'Try'—He undertakes several two-by-two combinations, but at random.

In contrast, the attempts of an older boy are systematic and exhaustive:

San. (12;3) . . . tries the four, and then each one independently, with g; then he spontaneously proceeds to various two by two combinations, writes them down and finds them all— He then adds drops and finds, yellow from $1 \times 3 \times g$ and says 'You need 1 and 3 and the drops.' He is then asked 'Where is the yellow, in there (g)?'—'No, they go together.'—'And 2?'—'I don't think it has any effect, it's water.'—'And 4?'—'It doesn't do anything either, it's water too. But I want to try again; you can't ever be too sure.' He proceeds systematically and finds the law, mixing $3 \times 1 \times g \times$ water, knowing that the five together gave no colour.

A child is satisfied when he has hit on a correct solution by trial and error or when he has verified his hypothesis, if he has one, on a single case; he does not conceive of a relationship taking a number of equivalent forms so he does not make tests to verify or exclude them. In other words, he does not conceive of a general law. But adolescents, such as Wak. (14;0) and Huc. (15;6) state their hypotheses as general laws which they test, and San. (12;3) considers every possibility, stating his result as a law.

This difference appears also in the expectations of children and adolescents. An adolescent quickly sees that several instances of a kind suggest the existence of a law which should hold good in all similar cases, but a child tends to see successive instances as separate, unrelated events. In Piaget's experiment (Piaget, 1960) with the angles of a triangle, for example, the familiar demonstration was made in which triangles were torn into three parts which were rearranged with the vertices adjacent to form a straight line. Young children did not learn from one instance to the next; they expected the angles to form now a straight line and now more or less than a straight line. Aug. (9;8) predicted results, saying 'It will be a semicircle,' in one case, but of the next, large triangle, he observed 'They'll be less because this angle (an acute angle in the right-angled triangle) isn't as big.' Having experimented he remarked, 'Oh no, it's a semicircle,' and of the next case he guessed 'Maybe that will be a semi-circle as well.' But Bed. (10;3) who has already reached the level of formal operations in this experiment, was certain that there could not be a triangle in which the angles did not make a semicircle. When shown three angles which together made more than 180° he asserted at once that they could not have come from the same triangle.

Perhaps it is the adolescent's capacity to expect to find general laws which enables him to recognize that an event may be a chance event, for he realizes that it may occur in a situation in which no law is operating. The young child's attitude is different; for him there are no laws with general application yet every event is explicable—the impossible can be imagined as a reality. A child at the pre-operational stage inquires 'If there was a tree in the middle of the lake, what would it do?' He agrees that there isn't one but adds 'I know there isn't, but if there was . . .' So he confuses the logical and the real order of things; his assumption is not a logical assumption but it has reality for him. In Piaget's words: 'The child is too much of a realist to be a logician, and too much of an intellectualist to be a pure observer.' During the period of concrete operations he becomes a better observer but reality still dominates logical possibilities; he never makes logical assumptions to see where they will lead and, if he has an imaginary model, he reasons directly from it, regarding it as real. Consequently there is still no room for chance. By contrast, the older adolescent, or adult, is sufficiently detached from his ego and from his inner world to be an objective observer, and simultaneously is sufficiently detached from external things to be able to reason about assumptions and hypotheses held as such; consequently he can establish general laws or note their absence when events occur randomly.

Definitions and symbolism

The different character of definitions given by adolescents is remarked on by Piaget but he gives no illustration of the exhaustive and general definitions characteristic of educated adolescents or adults. Use of the vocabulary tests in the Terman Merrill revision of the Binet tests, however, provides many examples. When asked the first question, 'What is orange? Tell me what orange means,' a young child usually answers 'To eat', referring only to its purpose relative to him; an older child may say, 'It's a fruit or a colour,' but an adolescent attempts to describe the general properties of the class of objects, or the category, known as orange. John, a bright boy aged 10;5, said, 'It's a kind of fruit, with a thin orange skin on top of white pith. Inside it's juicy. The juicy part is contained in a lot of sections—about eight or ten, I think, each one is in a thin skin. The whole fruit is rounded in shape, about two to four inches in diameter.' And he proceeded to try to define the colour before he considered that the question was adequately answered.

Similarly, in different situations, or in sayings, an adolescent seeks what is common to them in the most general terms. Whereas, in Chapter 5, we saw children looking for equivalents to proverbs by matching details, the arrangement of words for example, the adolescent's capacity to take different viewpoints enables him to see similarities in meaning; and he learns to make full use of similes and metaphor. His imagination is enriched by varied experiences and his powers of verbal expression are extended, enabling him to make allusions as well as assertions, but he does so within the limits of a logical possibility which replaces the illogical phantasy of childhood.

Continuity and infinity

Conceptions of continuity and infinity have been demonstrated by Piaget in questioning children about division of lines and shapes (Piaget, 1960). At the end of the subperiod of concrete operations children agree that a line may be subdivided many times, or that many points may be drawn on a line, but they believe that the division must cease at some finite number of parts and cannot imagine that the number of points may be increased indefinitely until they formed a straight line:

Gin. (10;4) asked to subdivide a square says 'The small-est possible square is a point'—'Has it a shape or not?'—'Round'—and of a subdivided line he is asked 'If one cuts this line without stopping?'—'You will finish with nothing at all.'—'And just before?'—'A fine line (*un trait*).'

and Bro. (10;5) says:

'The smallest possible square is like a point.'—'Really a point?'—'No, a point is smaller.'—'Go on.'—'It will be filled in the middle, it won't be a square any more.' When dividing a line he is asked 'Could we cut it again still more?'—'No, it's no more than a point.'—'How many points can you make between these two?'—'Thirty.'—'No more?'—'Yes.'—'Again more?'—'No, it will be a line.'—'But aren't a line and a lot of points the same?'—'No,' (hesitatingly)—'If one puts points all along?'—'That would make a line.'

The adolescents no longer insist on finite 'smallest sizes' and have no difficulty in thinking of indefinitely large numbers. To the question 'How many points could I put on this line?' Bet. (11;7) answers:

'One cannot say. They are innumerable. One could always make some smaller points.'—'About how many are there roughly?'—'It is impossible to say.'—'But approximately, ten thousand, one hundred thousand, a million?'—'It's impossible to say. One cannot say how many there are.'—'Make me the shortest line it is poss-ible to make.'—'No, one cannot, because it is always possible to make a still shorter one.'

and Duc. (12;9) sees at once that a line of points will be a continuous line if there is an indefinitely large number of them. These boys are no longer concerned to give a kind of reality to their points by insisting that they have shape, and it is of interest that Bet. says 'One cannot say.' Children will answer 'I don't know' but the assertion that it is not possible to say, or to know, does not appear until the level of formal operations is attained.

Relations between relations

The new capacity of the adolescent to deal with relations between relations has been demonstrated by Piaget and Inhelder in a variety of experiments involving proportionality, in problems which require consideration of all possible combinations or permutations of effects for their solution, in questions relating to conservation of volume and in estimates of correlation of attributes from their dispersal in sub-groups of a population.

In experimenting with the construction of similar figures (Piaget and Inhelder, 1956), Piaget found that children 'enlarged' a rectangle to 'one of similar shape' by lengthening it out of all proportion, but by stage IIIA they could take relative dimensions into account fairly accurately. At sub-stage IIIB their accuracy increased and, more important, they were increasingly aware of both dimensions of the rectangle as they made their comparisons; however, if the ratio was not a simple one, such as two or three times as large, they fell back on adding equal differences to the sides of the smaller shape. For example, Dan. (11;0) reasoned on a basis of differences so soon as the problem was difficult; but in stage IV the equality of ratios of length and breadth was generalized as a law.

The operations involved in understanding proportionality are described by Piaget in discussing Inhelder's experiments (Inhelder and Piaget, 1959). We will follow the argument, simply, in an experiment in which the shadows of a number of circular rings of different sizes were cast by a point of light onto a screen; the problem set to each child was to make the shadows coincide, firstly with two rings and, subsequently, with more—increasing to five or six. Let us suppose that a child has arranged one ring to cast a shadow on the screen and is deciding what to do with a different one. If he is capable of working it out he may argue as follows: 'If the shadow of the second ring is too big I can reduce it by moving the ring further from the light; if it is too small I can enlarge it by moving the ring nearer the light; alternatively, if the shadow is too big, I could replace the ring by a smaller one or, if it is too small I could replace the ring by a larger one.' So he takes into account four possible actions and, since he represents them mentally, we say he has considered four operations. However, to reach the level of formal operations he must not make any adjustments by trial and error, as children do, but must proceed by measurement with calculation of proportions. This 'group of four operations' occurs in all problems of proportionality as well as in other related problems. Piaget calls it 'The group of four transformations'. Readers who are interested in the description of the group in mathematical terms will find it in the references already given.

Piaget places the full development of the capacity to deal with such problems at about fourteen or fifteen years. Other experimenters confirm this. Mealings (op. cit.) set problems in which the weight of a rubber bung, and of a chain, could be obtained by fairly simple calculations by proportion after a few measurements were made. He found that pupils with M.A. of fifteen years or more all succeeded in the first; whereas in the second, M.A. was as high as fifteen years eight months before success was certain. Children with mental ages less than about thirteen years all failed.

Since understanding of proportionality is also required to achieve the concept of density, or to calculate equivalent volumes of different shapes, these concepts also appear at about the same mental age. To calculate density the ratios of two volumes and of two weights must be considered, although the calculation is customarily simplified by taking equal volumes and considering the ratio of weights only. We have already quoted Jim. (12;8) as saying 'If you take metal, you need much more wood to make the same weight as metal.' He does not know the convention so he takes equal weights and compares volumes.

A digression on a more fundamental misconception relating to conservation of volume which appears to persist into adolescence among a substantial number of children is of interest here. It suggests that they have failed to reach the level of concrete operations. In an experiment with a 'house' made of heavy bricks which was put under water (Piaget, 1960), first upright and then lying on its side, each child was asked, 'Is there the same amount of room in this house now as there was before?' Eti. (8;5) replied 'Yes, it's got the same bricks'—'And will it take up the same amount of room in the basin?'—'No, this way it's less'—'How do you explain that?'—'It's the same number of bricks but they take up less room.' So to him conservation of interior volume does not ensure conservation of the volume of water which is complementary. English children tested by members of the A.T.C.D.E. and their students, and by teachers (Beard, 1963), showed similar misconceptions. They were even more confused when objects of equal sizes but of different weights were to be put under water; many supposed that the heavier object would make the water rise much higher. The percentages of children able to answer correctly at different ages suggests that they lack practical experience in such problems throughout the primary school and that this deficiency is not always made good in the secondary schools even by pupils specializing in science.

Age in years and months	4·10-6·9	6·10-7·9	7·10-8·9	8·10	
Equal balls of different weights	8·6	19·1	3·2	9·4	%
Number of children tested	35	47	31	32	

In the study with older pupils the percentages were as follows:

Ages in years	7 & 8	9 & 10	11 & 12	13 & 14	15 & 16	
Equal tins of different weights	11·1	21·4	21·4	63·2	71·4	%
Number of children tested	10	14	14	19	14	

It should be noted that the sample of older children was biased as it contained unduly large numbers of children from grammar or selective secondary schools. Possibly these results cast some light on the avoidance by numerous candidates in the mathematics O-level papers of problems dealing with volumes and capacities.

Where calculation of volume was required e.g. replacement of a 'house' (dimensions $3 \times 3 \times 4$) by a 'house with equal room inside' on a base 2×3, proportionality was involved; Piaget found that children did not succeed until they were about twelve years old. Piaget et al. (1960). In a simple case such as this younger children sometimes succeeded by counting the total number of bricks.

Other problems can be set which involve forming relations between relations, but many can be reduced to the group of four transformations. Correlation, as tested by Piaget, is one such concept. To make his test he used cards with pictures of children belonging to four categories: fair hair with blue eyes, fair hair with brown eyes, brown hair with blue eyes, and brown hair with brown eyes. Lyn. (12;4) was shown a set of cards with (6, 0, 0, 6) in each category respectively and was asked 'Can you find a relation between hair and eye colour in the cards?'—'Yes, these (the dark ones) have the same colour eyes as hair.'—'No—here?'—'Here it's only brown.'—'And here?'—'It's blue, they are all blue.' 'And here (6, 2, 4, 4) is there a relationship?'—'No. Yes the four (subsets) separately, but not when they are together,'—'Why?'—'Because some are yellow (blond) and blue and some are yellow and brown.'

Her comparisons fall within one sub-category, here among the blonds. Vec. (14;6) at a later stage given sets (4, 2, 2, 4) and (3, 3, 1, 3) on each occasion compares the blue- and brown-eyed first among the blonds and then among the brunettes separately. Asked 'But for the whole set?' he replies 'There are 4/12 outside the law and 8/12 covered by it. It would be the same for the whole set.' Thus he is superior in his arguments to Lyn.

When asked to make classifications of the cards she easily does so. But when asked to make two groups so that the chances are higher, in one than in the other, of finding a relationship between hair and eye colour she gives (3, 4, 4, 4) and (3, 6, 6, 4); she organizes the sets correctly but she still justifies her arrangements by arguing about the first number as compared with the second or the third as compared with the fourth. She fails to see that she must consider the first and fourth together and the second and third together. Likewise, Bon. (14;3) limits his comparisons to one pair only. But Cog. (15;2) can state a law: 'most of the people with brown eyes have brown hair and most of those with blue eyes have blond hair.'

Mealings (op. cit.) found an identical incapacity to argue about sub-sets of different categories simultaneously. In an experiment in which some red and blue blocks had to be sorted into 'light' and 'heavy' ones, the light and heavy groups were of blocks roughly the same weights but distinctly different from each other. Among twenty-four boys and girls with mental ages less than fourteen and a half years only two succeeded in separating the two groups. Their difficulty was that they could not classify the blocks as 'about the same' or 'not about the same' and simultaneously classify with respect to the system as a whole. They would pronounce both of two blocks as 'light' 'because neither made the balance pan bang down', so illustrating the difficulty children have in dealing with relative terms before the level of formal operations is attained. When the separation into two groups was made for them into one red and two blue heavy ones and three red and two blue light ones, those with mental ages less than thirteen years eight months were unable to answer the question, 'Which are there more of, red blocks or light blocks?' for they could not cope with objects classified in two ways simultaneously.

A more complex way of forming relations between relations may be found in calculating probabilities based on permutations and combinations as well as on proportion. As we should expect, children do not attain the capacity to deal with such problems until their mental age is about fifteen or sixteen years. Piaget set some fairly simple problems in which children were asked to predict what colour ball was most likely to be drawn from a bag (Piaget and Inhelder, 1951). In one such experiment fourteen green balls, ten red, seven yellow and one blue ball were shown to the children and put into the bag; they were then asked which colours they would be most likely to draw if they took two. Gin. (10;10) predicted two green or one green and one yellow; after drawing two green ones, he predicted one green and one yellow next time; after drawing a yellow and a blue, he predicted that two red would be most likely. When asked 'Look at what has come out: has one more chance of reds or greens?' he replied 'Red, because there are already two green' (although 13 green ones remained), and he did not learn from subsequent experience or questions. Laur. (12;3), after drawing twice, gave a rule, 'It's always two green ones which have more chance,' but he failed to qualify his rule by saying how successive probabilities would depend on what was previously drawn.

This however, is a difficult problem; but in the experiment of combining liquids which we have already mentioned, they were able to form all the possible combinations. Even this simpler task involves forming relations between relations. Those who were successful built up all pairs of combinations of 1 with g, 2 with g, etc. and serialized the combinations: those with g, those with 1 etc., then proceeded systematically to serialize combinations, two at a time, three at a time, and so on.

One final example of thinking by an older adolescent must serve to show how the new capacities of formal operations may be used together to explore a problem exhaustively in a way far beyond the capacity of children. The problem (G.L.T.) is to determine why a metal bar attached to a non-metallic rotating disc always stops with the bar pointing to one pair of boxes instead of any of the other three pairs round the circumference of the disc. The boxes are placed, but not attached, on sectors of different colours and equal areas, each pair is marked with a distinct sign: diamond, oblong, circle or star.

Let us first see how a child reasons. Dup. (10;9) attempts to solve the problem by suggesting it is due to the weights, reverses the boxes with stars and circles, finds that the bar still stops at the starred boxes, and says, 'You can't do anything about it, it's always the same thing. It's complicated!' and finds no better procedure. The adolescent seeks every possibility, expresses each in terms of a hypothesis which he proceeds systematically to test, altering just one variable at a time: Gon. (14;11) reasons as follows, 'Maybe it goes down and here it's heavier (the weight might lower the plane, thus resulting in the needle's coming to rest at the lowest point) or maybe there's a magnet (he puts a notebook under the board to level it, and sees that the result is the same)'—'What have you proved?'—'There is a magnet' (he weighs the boxes). 'There are some that are heavier than others (more or less heavy). I think it's more likely to be the content (in substance)'—'What do you have to do to prove that it isn't the weight?'—He removes the boxes marked with diamonds which are the heaviest, saying, 'Then I changed positions. If it stops at

III

the same place again, the weight doesn't play any role. But I would rather remove the starred boxes. We'll see whether it stops at the others which are heavier (experiments). It's not the weight. It's not a rigorous proof, because it does not come to rest at the perpendicular (to the boxes with diamonds). The weight could only have an effect if it made the plane tip. So I'll put two boxes one on top of the other and if it doesn't stop that means that the weight doesn't matter (negative experiment). You see.' —'And the colour?' 'No, you saw when the positions of the boxes was changed. The content of the boxes has an effect, but it's especially when the boxes are close together, the boxes are only important when they are close (he puts half of the boxes at a greater distance). It's either the distance or the content. To see whether it's the content I'm going to do this (he moves the starred boxes away and moves the others closer). The pointer then falls exactly between the round ones which are near and the starred ones which are far off. Both things have an effect and it's the result of two forces (an experiment in which the starred boxes moved away by successive steps). It's more likely to be distance (new trial). It seems to be confirmed, but I'm not quite sure. Unless it's the cardinal points. (He takes off the starred boxes.) No, it's not that. The stars do have an effect. It must be the content. If it isn't a magnet I don't see what it could be. You have to put iron on the other boxes. If the magnet is there (disc), it will come to these boxes. If it is in the boxes (stars) there is iron under the disc (he removes the starred boxes). I'm sure that it's in the boxes.'

In reading this excellent analysis of the problem the reader will probably question whether the majority of fifteen-year-olds (or adults) could do as well. Evidently this boy is highly intelligent and has been trained to think scientifically. Many adults do not attain the level of formal operations except in some limited areas; if they are neither well educated nor of good intelligence they may hardly reach it at all. In societies where few adults have received schooling the only evidence of formal thinking among the majority of the population may well be in their understanding of proverbs and in some attempts to generalize meaning. The problem for the teacher is to use teaching methods in such a way as to maximize developments of formal thinking wherever it is possible.

Implications for Secondary School teachers

Piaget's contribution to the study of the development of thinking during adolescence is, perhaps, of even more value than his observations and experiments of the thinking of younger children. In England and America a number of psychologists had made substantial contributions to our understanding of children's early mental development before Piaget's work was known and this had already resulted in Nursery and Infants' Schools using apparatus and active methods in teaching, while in Junior Schools in England a similar development has taken place with increasing momentum during the last ten years or so. In the Secondary Schools, however, the rate of change has been slower and a substantial part of teaching still proceeds on lines laid down in Grammar Schools as long as thirty or forty years ago. It is true that modifications in teaching methods have been brought about by teachers' associations and as a result of recommendations from University Departments of Education or the Training Colleges and, recently, new programmes of mathematics and science teaching have been introduced in some schools, but the influence of innovations has been less marked than in schools for younger children. Even the introduction of new types of schools has had more effect on curricula than on methods. This may be partly because little more than half the graduate teachers have been trained to teach, but even more to the fact that experiments tend to be taken up only by individual enthusiasts or by small groups of teachers. Yet

Piaget's findings and those of other psychologists working on similar lines suggest that considerable changes in teaching methods would be desirable at this level also.

In the first place, experiments in Birmingham (Mealings, 1963, and Peel, 1960) have shown that the capacity for thinking in formal operations does not develop until children attain a mental age of about thirteen years. From this it follows that teaching methods for the majority of pupils in the first two years in secondary school, and even later for those who are backward, should be suited to children who think in concrete terms.

Since many concepts have still to be acquired throughout the secondary stage, it follows also from Piaget's findings that when beginning a new topic learning should be based on concrete experiences or on the children's (or adolescents') own experiences even in the case of the most able pupils. This has, of course, been recognized by some teachers for many years. The Mathematical Association's Report on the Teaching of Geometry (1956) for example suggests three levels of approach : stage A, consisting of experimental geometry, stage B, a deductive stage in which the interest lies in the search for geometrical truths and stage C, the systematizing stage, in which much of the interest is transferred to the way in which these truths are linked together. The committee which prepared the 1938 report introduced the first of these stages, for, they said 'one of the great mistakes in the teaching of Mathematics, and one to which we are always liable, is that of presenting abstractions familiar to ourselves to minds unprepared for them'. They also stressed the importance of ensuring that the children did the work '. . . boys should be left to attempt the questions in the first instance unaided; the reading of the question and its translation first into a free-hand sketch to discover the meaning and then into a measured drawing, are the most important parts of the exercise for the boys and should on no account be done for them'. Thus, these enlightened teachers already recognized that even highly intelligent children in the secondary grammar schools required a transition stage in learning when meeting new subjects and that they needed to learn to translate from verbal description to other forms of representation.

In fact, as O-level examiners well know, there are still many ways in which children as old as sixteen years fail to translate concrete experiences into verbal descriptions and other forms of representation, or vice versa, or from one kind of representation to another; there are also many concepts which are not essentially too difficult for juniors to learn which are still not mastered. For example, O-level candidates commonly find it difficult to draw representations of three-dimensional figures. In the case of a sphere resting on a square frame composed of four rods they would, no doubt, have known what to expect if they had been given the materials to put together, but they could not imagine it and then represent it; a large number of candidates drew a sphere standing on a plane defined by the rods while others seemed to have no conception at which points the sphere would touch the rods. It seems reasonably certain that these children lacked experience of making or using models and of drawing them and then describing the relationships they observed. Similar failures to translate from experience into various forms of representation (or conversely) occur in most other subjects, whether in understanding proverbs and metaphors, in developing moral concepts, summing up general laws in formulae or learning principles in science. Too often children begin from the wrong end in learning. They are provided with quantities of information but too little time is employed in discussing its relation to their own problems, in eliciting what they have partly realized, or in helping them to understand concepts and principles through their attempts to represent and to understand their own experiments or observations.

A problem of another kind, as Vigotsky (1962) has

pointed out, is that although adolescents form and use many concepts correctly they may, nevertheless, find them strangely difficult to express in words, for concepts often evolve unconsciously. In such cases discussion may suffice to make conscious what has been implicitly realized. In studying history, for example, many terms will have been met and used appropriately as a result of general reading and listening but attempts to define them may present considerable difficulty at first and may uncover incomplete understanding and minor misconceptions. In learning concepts Vigotsky stresses the need for problems: '. . . memorizing words and connecting them with objects does not in itself lead to concept formation; for the process to begin, a problem must arise that cannot be solved otherwise than through the formation of new concepts.' The most inquiring minds generate their own problems so that information provided is readily assimilated, but for the majority of pupils the teacher must present the subject matter as a problem. Thus if we present a map showing contours, rivers, and the location of natural resources, relevant concepts are more likely to be learned if we ask pupils to decide where the towns should be, and to substantiate their views, than if the towns are included from the beginning and an account of their growth is read, or reasons why they were sited where they were, are expounded by the teacher. The latter presents no problems and makes little demands on the pupils' thinking. When most of teaching and the environment fails to present appropriate problems Vigotsky believes that thinking fails to reach the highest stages or reaches them with great delay. In this, of course, he agrees with Piaget, who believes that capacity for thinking in formal operations is initiated by problems raised in attempting to reconcile different viewpoints in discussion and co-operative tasks.

It may well be questioned whether discussion between pupils is used sufficiently, or sufficiently skilfully, in our secondary schools. Much class discussion consists in questions and answers between the teacher and individual pupils, and this may fail to provide the genuine exchange of viewpoints needed for the development of logical thinking, since the teacher inevitably tends to be accepted as an authority. Even at university level the quality of students' thinking in their own subjects may still only partly attain the level of formal operations, despite Piaget's finding that thinking at this level is normally more fully achieved at sixteen years; but this seems to have been an optimistic conclusion based on studies of rather few and perhaps unrepresentative samples of adolescents. Observations and experiments by Abercrombie (1960), with first-year university students in London showed that although they were well-grounded in the facts of biology, physics and chemistry they were often unable to use their information to solve slightly unfamiliar problems or to defend a view in argument, and they tended to observe what the textbook said should be there rather than what was actually on a slide or X-ray. To overcome these deficiencies she experimented with free discussion among small groups of students of their own observations, definitions, evaluation of evidence or views on causation. In this way they became aware, to the dismay of some of them, that they made unconscious assumptions, took individual views of the same evidence or saw different features of an exhibit. Subsequently, students who had taken part in these discussions were compared with those who had attended the normal course of lectures and demonstrations: they discriminated better between facts and conclusions, drew fewer false inferences, considered more than one solution and were less adversely influenced in their approach to a problem by their experience of the preceding one. The discussion method, therefore, promoted a more scientific attitude by giving rise to more objective and flexible behaviour than did learning the facts of science by traditional methods. The implications for teachers of sixth-form sciences are obvious; but we may reasonably assume that these findings have applications in any subject, or at any age, where critical thinking is required.

The reader who is interested in the bearing of emotional development on thinking will find that Piaget admits its importance but has neglected to investigate its effects. Adolescence is, however, a time when pupils are likely to be much concerned with emotional problems of personality development and, if these are sufficiently severe, they may well regress in their thinking to an earlier stage. Where teaching methods are used that are inappropriate to their level of development this, in itself, adds to their emotional difficulties by denying them the satisfaction of interest and success which follow when appropriate methods are used.

Concluding remarks

The foregoing account of Piaget's investigations suffices to show that his findings are a challenge to teachers at all levels to look again at their methods of teaching in relation to the development of their pupils' thinking. In addition, they suggest solutions to some of the problems which arise in teaching. There are four main aspects of development during school years to which Piaget has drawn attention: the directive function of language, the formation of concepts, translation of concrete experiences into verbal and symbolic terms and the evolution of logical thinking. As children grow up the emphasis will be greater on one or other of these developments, but all of them are represented in some degree throughout schooling and higher education.

Although Piaget's work suggests many new approaches in teaching, this has not been his main concern; his object has been to describe children's thinking, not to improve it. If teachers are to use his findings to the best advantage further experimental work is needed in order to find the most effective methods of teaching. Of the four aspects of

development in thinking mentioned above only the formation of concepts has been at all fully explored and even in
this case there is still much to do. So far, no one has made
longitudinal studies of groups of children to see in what
way understanding of concepts develops throughout school
life, nor have new teaching methods been objectively tested
to see whether, or in what ways, they advance children's
capacity to form concepts or to think logically. Some of
these gaps may be closed in a few years' time. For example,
teachers in one region from groups of schools using 'discovery' and 'traditional' methods to teach mathematics
are testing their pupils to see how their ability to form
mathematical concepts develops under the two different
treatments. Since the samples are large, variations due to
teaching ability or to socio-economic status of the children's homes should be roughly equal and differences in
achievement may therefore be attributed to differences in
teaching methods. It should also enable the teachers to
explore differences in development of individual children
in relation to such factors as the status of the home, sex
or personality type and to discover any interaction there
may be between teaching methods and age.

An attitude of accepting experiments as an essential part
of the evaluation of teaching methods needs to be fostered.
Repetition of Piaget's own experiments is instructive to
students or to teachers who have never used them.
Students report that they would not have believed that
children could have such misconceptions if they had not
seen what they did and heard their explanations; but
teachers who have already used some of the experiments
as they were originally designed would do well to experiment by varying questions, using different materials, or
trying simple teaching experience to see in what way
these influence results.

Development of the directive function of language begins, as we have seen, in the Nursery School years but
once developed it continues in use throughout life. The

university student who performs some practical activity, such as a dissection, or a cook following a recipe, also use language to direct their activities although in these cases it is possible for them to follow the instructions in silence, and perhaps to recall them later without the intermediary of tape or print. However, teachers in secondary schools will be well aware that some pupils are unable to follow printed instructions, except of the simplest kinds, and this raises the problem as to how they could be helped to do so. At this point, Piaget's investigations are of no assistance; it is essential to explore new approaches in teaching —such as programmed learning, films, tape linked with programmes, discussions or children's written descriptions of their own actions—until methods are found which are more effective in enabling them to follow written instructions provided by other people.

Nevertheless, we should be careful not to verbalize where it is unnecessary. In learning new concepts, for example, it is better initially to 'see' a common property or relationship and only later to describe it; and in learning some skills we 'see' how to perform them from a demonstration and can repeat the actions ourselves far more rapidly without the interference of words. It seems that we have a mental capacity to see or to imitate actions immediately, as a whole (or in very swift succession), whereas language analyses serially and too slowly and so interferes with our spontaneous synthesis. Of course this ability could arise from earlier experience of guiding actions by words, but imitation of gestures by infants and by the deaf suggests that it need not.

Ability to translate concrete experiences into verbal and symbolic terms seems to be one essential factor in attainment of formal operations; but Piaget provides little guidance as to how to attain it. Certainly discussions should help. But what kind of discussion and how should it be organized? Or should we use the more systematic methods of Talyzina and Galparin (1961) who gradually superseded activities with verbal directions repeated mentally? Or, again, might we explore some kind of programmed learning in which increasingly complex verbal directions could be used to guide self-correcting activities? This already suggests a wide field for further exploration; but when we add the use of formulae, diagrams, models and pictures, or mime perhaps, which may represent relationships of different kinds as well as (or more tersely than) words, we have an area of learning and thinking which is almost wholly unexplored. A formula, for example, summarizes relationships very concisely and, although it is a kind of shorthand, it is not meant to be translated into the more cumbrous verbal expression of the law it states; but the introduction of some children to formulae is such that they prefer a verbal statement, however long, to interpreting a few symbols. Diagrams and models are essentially visual, or kinaesthetic but, like formulae, may summarize relationships succinctly where a verbal description would be tediously long. All of these forms of representation must play a part in attaining different aspects of logical thinking; but, whereas formulae, diagrams and models, as well as verbal expression, are important to students of science and mathematics, verbal expression alone can suffice for students of the arts, while television and drama probably play a large part in assisting less able or less well-educated individuals to enter into other people's experiences and so to attain an appreciation of different viewpoints which Piaget believes to be the initial step in attainment of formal operations. Perhaps, therefore, the emphasis Piaget gives to verbal communication is too great. This is, of course, the traditional emphasis in schools and in much of our society; but it seems desirable that the role of other methods of representation in advancing formal operations should be explored as well as means to aid pupils in translating from one form of representation to another.

If we use teaching methods to develop all these aspects of thinking it seems probable that we shall find that our pupils attain the various levels of thinking far earlier than formerly. We have but to compare the thinking of un-educated adults from primitive societies with that of older children in our schools to see the kind of advances which a stimulating environment and teaching can achieve. To attain considerable advances we need to systematize ex-ploration of children's learning and thinking, including those aspects which have been relatively neglected, and to develop new approaches to teaching based on a fuller knowledge of children's differences in mental develop-ment. This will take some years to achieve. Meanwhile, if we apply only what we have realized from Piaget's investi-gations, learning to think logically should become a more agreeable pursuit for the majority of children and we may expect to see substantial advances in their capacity to do so.

Bibliography

ABERCROMBIE, M. L. J. (1960), *The Anatomy of Judgment*, London: Hutchinson.

ANASTASI, A. (1958), *Differential Psychology*, New York: Macmillan (3rd edition).

ASSOCIATION OF TEACHERS IN COLLEGES AND DEPARTMENTS OF EDUCATION, MATHEMATICS SECTION (1963), *Primary Mathematics for Schools and Training Colleges*, London: A.T.C.D.E. (151 Gower Street, London, W.C.1.).

BAYLEY, N. (1933), *Mental Growth During the First Three Years*, Genetic Psychology Monographs, xiv.

BEARD, R. M. (1960), 'The nature and development of concepts, II', *Educational Review*, xiii (1960), 12-26.

BEARD, R. M. (1963), 'The order of concept development: studies in two fields', *Educational Review*, xv (1963), 105-117, 228-237.

BEARD, R. M. (1964), 'Further studies in concept development', *Educational Review*, xvii (1964), 41-58.

BEARD, R. M. (1965), 'Educational research and the learning of mathematics' in *Aspects of Education II: A New Look in Mathematics Teaching*, edited by Land, F. (*Journal of the Institute of Education*, University of Hull), (1965), 32-45.

BEARD, R. M. (1968), 'An Investigation into Mathematical Concepts among Ghanaian Children I', *Teacher Education*, May, 1968.

BIBLIOGRAPHY

BERNSTEIN, B. (1961), 'Social structure, language and learning', *Educational Research*, iii (1961), 163-176.

BIGGS, J. M. (1962), *Anxiety, Motivation and Primary School Mathematics*, National Foundation for Educational Research (The Mere, Upton Park, Slough, Bucks.).

CENTRAL ADVISORY COMMITTEE FOR EDUCATION (1967), (Chairman: Lady Plowden), *Children and their Primary Schools*, London: H.M.S.O., 1967.

DAVIS, E. A. (1937), *The development of linguistic skill in twins, singletons with siblings and only children from age five to ten years*, University of Minnesota, Institute of Child Welfare, Monograph Series, No. 14.

DEUTSCHE, J. M. (1937), *The Development of Children's Concepts of Causal Relations*, University of Minnesota, Institute of Child Welfare, Monograph Series, No. 13.

DIENES, Z. P. (1964), *Building up Mathematics*, London: Hutchinson.

ELLIS, H. (1904), *A Study of British Genius*, London: Hunt and Blackett.

FLAVELL, J. H. (1963), *The Developmental Psychology of Jean Piaget*, New York: Van Nostrand.

FORGUS, R. (1954), 'The effect of early perceptual learning on the behavioural organisation of adult rats', *Journal of Comparative Physiological Psychology*, xlvii (1954), 331-336.

GALPARIN, P. YA and TALYZINA, N. F. (1961), 'Formation of elementary pupils' in *Recent Soviet Psychology*, edited by O'Connor, N., New York: Pergamon Press.

GARDNER, D. E. M. (1950), *Testing Results in the Infant School*, London: Methuen.

GOLDFARB, W. (1955), 'Emotional and intellectual consequences of psychologic deprivation in infancy: a revaluation', in *Psychopathology of Childhood*, edited by Hoch, P. H. and Zubin, J., New York: Grune & Stralton.

HARLOW, H. F. (1959), 'Love in infant monkeys', *Scientific American*, June 1959.

HAYES, K. J. and HAYES, C. (1951), 'The intellectual develop-
124

ment of a home-raised chimpanzee', *Proceedings of the American Philosophical Society*, XCV (1951), 105-109.

HOOD, H B. (1962), 'An experimental study of Piaget's theory of the development of number in children', *British Journal of Psychology*, liii (1962), 273-286.

HUNT, J. MCV. (1961), *Intelligence and Experience*, New York : Ronald Press.

HYDE, D. M. (1959), *An Investigation of Piaget's theories of the Concept of Number*, unpublished Ph.D. thesis, University of London.

INHELDER, B. and PIAGET, J. (1959), *The Growth of Logical Thinking*, London : Routledge & Kegan Paul.

ISAACS, S. (1932), *The Children We Teach*, University of London Press.

LOVELL, K. (1961), *The Growth of Basic Mathematical and Scientific Concepts in Children*, University of London Press.

LURIA, A. R. (1959), 'Development of the directive function of speech', *Word*, xv (1959), 341-352.

LURIA, A. R. (1961), *The Role of Speech in the Regulation of Normal and Abnormal Behaviour*, London: Pergamon Press.

LURIA, A. R. and YUDOVICH, F. IA. (1966), *Speech and Development of Mental Processes in the Child*, London ı Staples Press (2nd Impression).

MCFIE, J. (1961), 'The effect of education on African performance on a group of intellectual tests', *British Journal of Educational Psychology*, xxxi (1961), 232-240.

MATHEMATICAL ASSOCIATION (1956), *The Teaching of Mathematics in Primary Schools*, London : Bell.

MAYS, W. (1955), 'How we form concepts', *Science News*, XXXV (1955), 11-23.

MEAD, M. (1932), 'An investigation of the thought of primitive children with special reference to animism', *Journal of the Royal Anthropological Institute of Great Britain and Ireland*, lxii (1932), 173-190.

MEALINGS, R. J. (1963), 'Problem-solving in science teaching', *Educational Review*, xv (1963), 194-207.

NELSON, S. A. (1962), *An Investigation into the Relationship between the Level of Number Concepts held and Attainment in an E.S.N. School*, unpublished D. E. Dissertation, University of Bristol.

OAKES, M. E. (1947), *Children's Explanations of Natural Phenomena*, in *Contributions to Education*, No. 926, Teachers' College, Columbia University, 1947.

PARSONS, C. (1960), 'Inhelder and Piaget's "The Growth of Logical Thinking", II: A Logician's Viewpoint', review article in *British Journal of Psychology*, li (1960), 75-84.

PEEL, E. A. (1960), *The Pupil's Thinking*, London: Oldbourne.

PEEL, E. A. (1966), 'A study of differences in the judgments of adolescent pupils', *British Journal of Educational Psychology*, xxxvi (1966), 77-86.

PIAGET, J. (1926), *The Language and Thought of the Child*, London: Routledge & Kegan Paul.

PIAGET, J. (1928), *Judgment and Reasoning in the Child*, London: Routledge & Kegan Paul.

PIAGET, J. (1929), *The Child's Conception of the World*, London: Routledge & Kegan Paul.

PIAGET, J. (1930), *The Child's Conception of Physical Causality*, London: Routledge & Kegan Paul.

PIAGET, J. (1932), *The Moral Judgment of the Child*, London: Routledge & Kegan Paul.

PIAGET, J. (1946a), *Les Notions du Mouvement et de la Vitesse chez l'Enfant*, Paris: Presses Universitaires de France.

PIAGET, J. (1946b), *Le Developpement de la Notion de Temps chez l'Enfant*, Paris: Presses Universitaires de France.

PIAGET, J. (1950), *The Psychology of Intelligence*, London: Routledge & Kegan Paul.

PIAGET, J. (1951), *Play, Dreams and Imitation in Childhood*, London: Heinemann.

PIAGET, J. (1953a), *The Origins of Intelligence in the Child*, London: Routledge & Kegan Paul.

PIAGET, J. (1953b), *Logic in Psychology*, Manchester University Press.

PIAGET, J. (1955), *The Child's Construction of Reality*, London: Routledge & Kegan Paul.

PIAGET, J. et al. (1956), *Le Problème des Stades en Psychologie de l'Enfant*, Symposium de l'Association Psychologique de Langue Française, Paris: Presses Universitaires de France.

PIAGET, J. et al. (1960), *The Child's Conception of Geometry*, London: Routledge & Kegan Paul.

PIAGET, J. and INHELDER, B. (1941), *Le Developpement des Quantites chez l'Enfant*, Paris: Delachaux & Niestlé.

PIAGET, J. and INHELDER, B. (1951), *La Genèse de l'idée de Hazard chez l'Enfant*, Paris: Presses Universitaires de France.

PIAGET, J. and INHELDER, B. (1956), *The Child's Conception of Space*, London: Routledge & Kegan Paul.

PIAGET, J. and INHELDER, B. (1959) *La Genèse des Structures Logiques Elementaires*, Paris: Delachaux & Niestlé.

PIAGET, J. and SZEMINSKA, A. (1952), *The Child's Conception of Number*, London: Routledge & Kegan Paul.

REY, A., in PIAGET, J. (1950), *The Psychology of Intelligence*, London: Routledge & Kegan Paul.

RUSSELL, R. W. and DENNIS, W. (1939), 'Studies in Animism I: A Standardised Procedure for the Investigation of Animism', *Journal of Genetic Psychology*, lv (1939), 55-7.

SCHOOLS COUNCIL FOR THE CURRICULUM AND EXAMINATIONS (1965), *Mathematics in Primary Schools*, Curriculum Bulletin 1, London: H.M.S.O.

SPITZ, R. A. (1945), 'Hospitalism. An Inquiry into the genesis of psychiatric conditions in early childhood', *Psychoanalytic Study of the Child*, i (1945), 53-74, 113-117.

TANNER, J. M. (1963), 'Physical Development' in *Studies in Education: First Years in School*, edited by Brearley, M., London: Evans Bros.

TANSLEY, A. E. and GULLIFORD, R. (1965), *The Education of*

Slow Learning Children, London: Routledge & Kegan Paul.

THOMPSON, W. R. and HERON, W. (1954), 'The effects of restricting early experience on the problem-solving capacity of rats', *Canadian Journal of Psychology*, viii (1954), 17-31.

VALENTINE, C. W. (1942), *The Psychology of Early Childhood, A Study of Mental Development in the First Years of Life*, London: Methuen.

VERNON, M. D. (1962), *The Psychology of Perception*, London: Penguin Books.

VERNON, P. E. (1963), 'Experimental handicaps and intellectual development', *British Journal of Educational Psychology*, xxxiii (1963), 9-20, 117-126.

VERNON, P. E. (1966), 'Educational and intellectual development among Canadian Indians and Eskimos', *Educational Review*, xviii (1966), 79-91, 186-195.

VIGOTSKY, L. S. (1962), *Thought and Language*, New York: Wiley and Massachusetts Institute of Technology.

WALLACE, J. G. (1965), *Concept Growth and the Education of the Child*, National Foundation for Educational Research (The Mere, Upton Park, Slough, Bucks.). Occasional Publication Series, No. 12.

WALTER, W. GREY (1961), *The Living Brain*, London: Penguin Books.

WALTER, W. GREY (1956), in *Discussions on Child Development*, edited by Tanner, J. M. and Inhelder, B. (The proceedings of the first meeting of the W.H.O. Study Group on the psychological development of the Child), London: Tavistock Press.